House OF Lisabeth
Design Magazine

Summer Days and
Summer NIghts

18

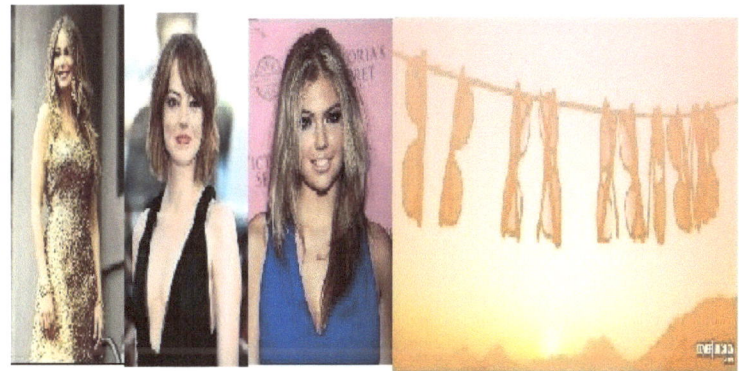

16 of July's Most Sizzling Summers Hotties
Ladies Edition

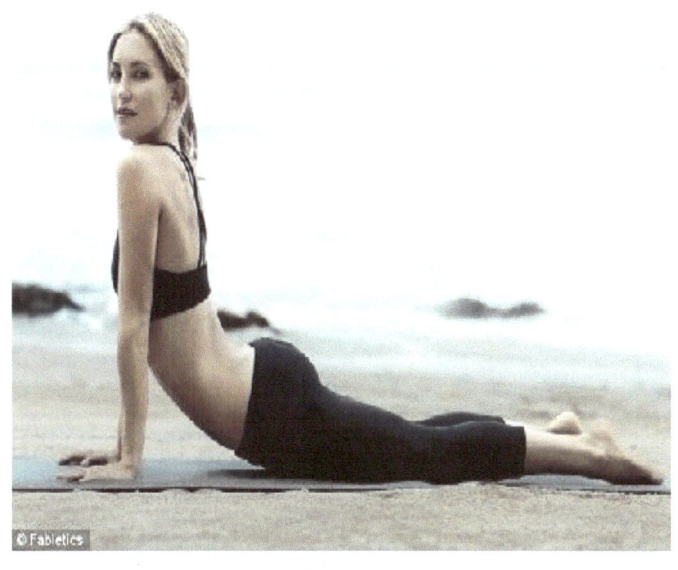

Fashion News
And Updates:

Tips On Beating The Heat..
Find Out How To Beat That
Heat Stroke

13

Tremdy News What
You Want To Know

23

Opinions Section:
15 Signs You'll Be Rich

5

Design & Concepts L.L.C
July 2015 Issue

House of:
Lisabeth Design
Magazine

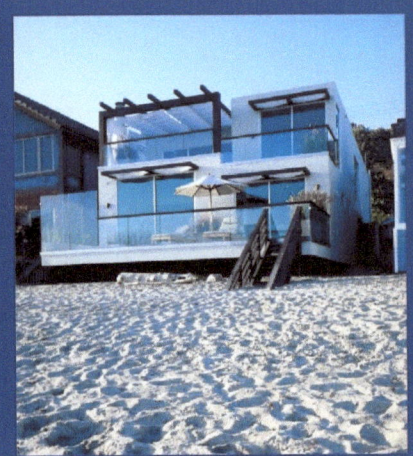

Today's Issue:

- *Doggy's world*
- *Fashion No's*
- *Design or Not*
- *Featured Business*

House of Lisabeth Design Magazine 2015

•HEALTH TRENDS
•WHATS GOING ON
•DOGGY'S WORLD
•THE BUZZ
•FASHION NO OR NOT-
FASHION THIS OR FASH-
ION THAT
•NIGHTLIFE
LISABETH DESIGN
•DESIGN THIS-
•TRENDY OF 2014-UP TO
THE MINUTE
• *Classifieds*
• *Opinion Sections*
 2015– and more
•LIVE EVENTS
WHATS WHO, WHOS WHAT
•FEATURED BUSINESS:
BUSINESS OF- YESTER-
DAY, -TODAY, AND TOMOR-
ROW
•(ARIZONA, LA, LV, and
more! EVENT(S)
•POLICTICS
TRANSFORMED
•FIND US!
CALENDER

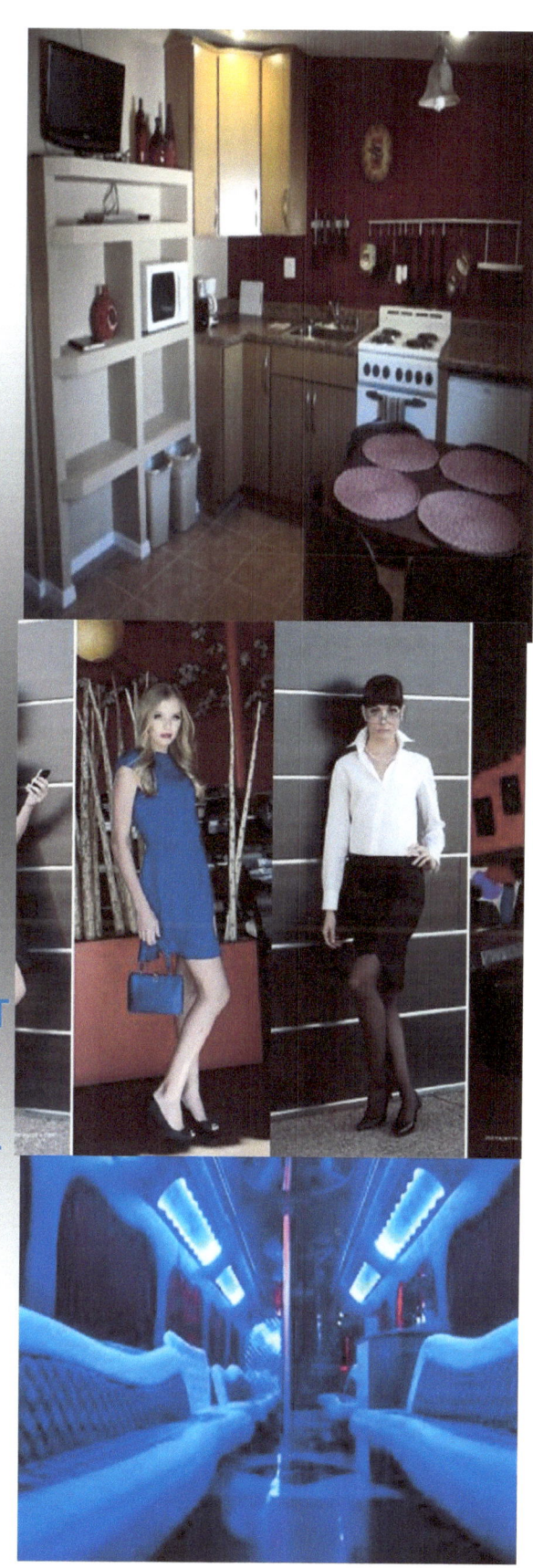

Health Watch

Tips on beating that heat stroke

What is a heat stroke?   Heatstroke is a condition caused by your body overheating, usually as a result of prolonged exposure to or physical exertion in high temperatures. This most serious form of heat injury, heatstroke can occur if your body temperature rises to 104 F (40 C) or higher.

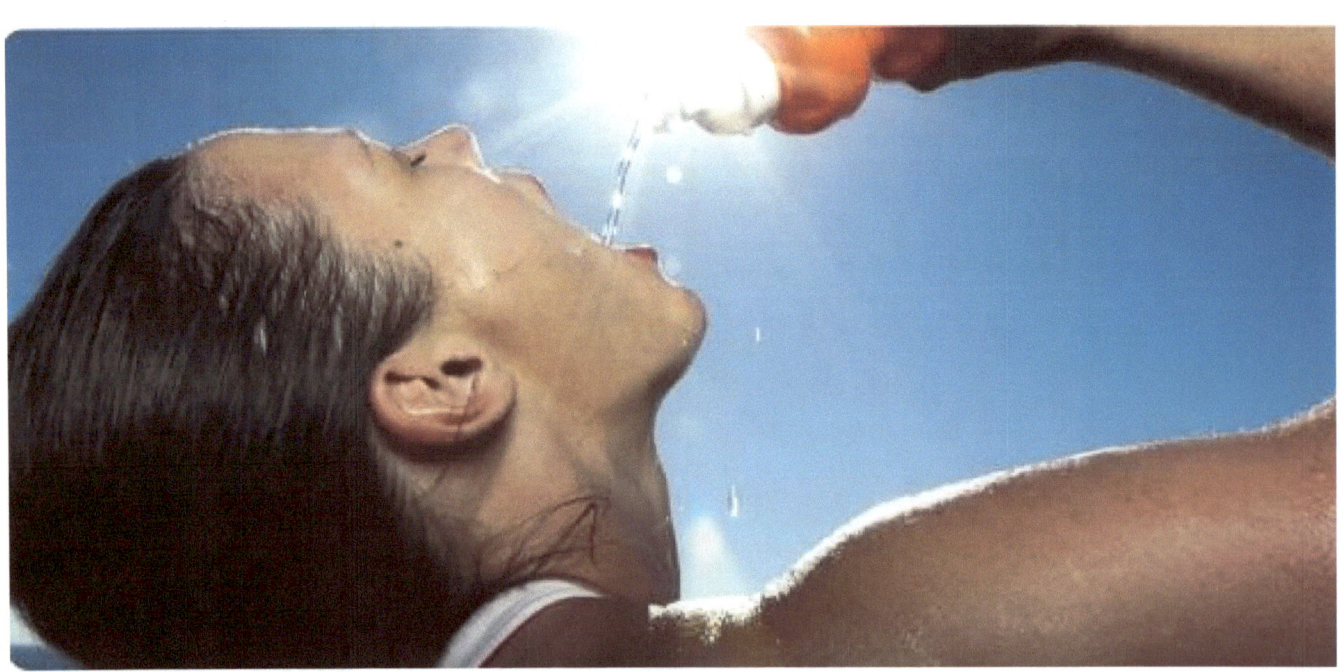

Heatstroke symptoms include:

High body temperature. A body temperature of 104 F (40 C) or higher is the main sign of heatstroke.

Altered mental state or behavior. Confusion, agitation, slurred speech, irritability, delirium, seizures and coma can all result from heatstroke.

Alteration in sweating. In heatstroke brought on by hot weather, your skin will feel hot and dry to the touch. However, in heatstroke brought on by strenuous exercise, your skin may feel moist.

Nausea and vomiting. You may feel sick to your stomach or vomit.

Flushed skin. Your skin may turn red as your body temperature increases.

Rapid breathing. Your breathing may become rapid and shallow.

Racing heart rate. Your pulse may significantly increase because heat stress places a tremendous burden on your heart to help cool your body.

Headache. Your head may throb.

When finding your self experienceing anything you might want to get out of the sun. Also Heatstroke requires emergency treatment. Untreated heatstroke can quickly damage your brain, heart, kidneys and muscles. The damage worsens the longer treatment is delayed, increasing your risk of serious complications or death.

Heatstroke can result in a number of complications, depending on how long the body temperature is high. Severe complications include:

Vital organ damage. Without a quick response to lower body temperature, heatstroke can cause your brain or other vital organs to swell, possibly resulting in permanent damage.

Death. Without prompt and adequate treatment, heatstroke can be fatal.

Opinions Section: 15 Signs You'll Be Rich

1. Attractive men earn 9 percent more money than unattractive men; attractive women earn 4 percent more money than unattractive women.

"There is a significant penalty for bad looks among men," write the economists whose research yielded these statistics. "Men who are viewed as being below average or homely are penalized" when it comes to wages. Noting that many studies have been done on workplace discrimination against women and ethnic minorities, these scholars undertook "the first study of the economics of discrimination in the labor market against yet another group—the ugly."

Daniel S. Hamermesh and Biddle, Jeff E. (1994): Beauty and the Labor Market. American Economic Review, 84 (5), 1174-1194.

2. Individuals with above-average IQs are only 1.2 times as likely as individuals with below-average IQs to have a high net worth.

3. People who were popular in high school earn 10 percent more than people who weren't.

Popularity pays, according to a study examining the effects of what academics call "friendship nomination"—that is, how many people claim you as their friends, not how many people you claim as friends

4. Graduates of Princeton University and Dartmouth College earn salaries 162 percent higher, on average, than graduates of East Texas Baptist University.

5. For every three inches taller than average they are, women earn 5 to 8 percent more money than women of average height; men earn 4 to 10 percent more for every extra three inches in height.

The study that includes these figures was done in Australia, where the premiums for added height are only about half of those in the U.S., according to the authors.

6. Being married and staying married increases your net worth by 77 percent.

Divorced people "experience an average wealth drop of 77 percent," according to the study that yielded this stat, and married people's "wealth increases on average 16 percent per each year of marriage."

7. Drinkers earn 10 to 14 percent more money than abstainers.

"Drinking leads to higher earnings by increasing social capital," write the researchers whose work yielded this stat.

8. Those who earned undergraduate degrees in petroleum engineering earn salaries over four times as high as those who earned undergraduate degrees in child and family studies.

9. Each one-unit increase in a typical young person's body mass index is associated with an 8 percent reduction in wealth.

10. 22 percent of American households headed by persons of Russian ancestry have a net worth of $1 million or more.

11. 21 percent of white Americans and only 2 percent of African Americans and 8 percent of Hispanics buy real estate or make other investments at young ages, which economists consider a key predictor of future wealth.

12. Blond women earn 7 percent more money than non-blonds.

And blond women marry men who earn about 6 percent more than the husbands of non-blonds, according to the study that yielded this stat. Blond hair is

13. Nonsmokers' net worth is about 50 percent higher than that of light smokers, and more than twice as much as that of heavy smokers.

14. 36 percent of American children born to parents in the uppermost economic bracket remain there as adults.

15. 54 percent of American children who are born to parents in the uppermost economic bracket and who then earn college degrees remain at the top.

DESIGN SEO STYLE CREATE SEO LIFE

The table at which I am sitting measures 75 centimetres by 90 centimetres, which, anywhere else, would be a table for four. At the new Kent Street Kitchen, however, it's a table for two. Everything here is big. It's like dining in the Land of the Giants. After a four-month renovation, the rooms that once housed The Observatory's formal 60-seater Galileo restaurant and Library Bar now form one long room the size of an auditorium, seating 140. Floral displays are enormous; chandeliers, gigantic.

That's what happens when a luxury hotel group such as The Langham moves to sunny Sydney. More accustomed to Hong Kong's high rents or London's tight squeeze on space, it's spreading its wings

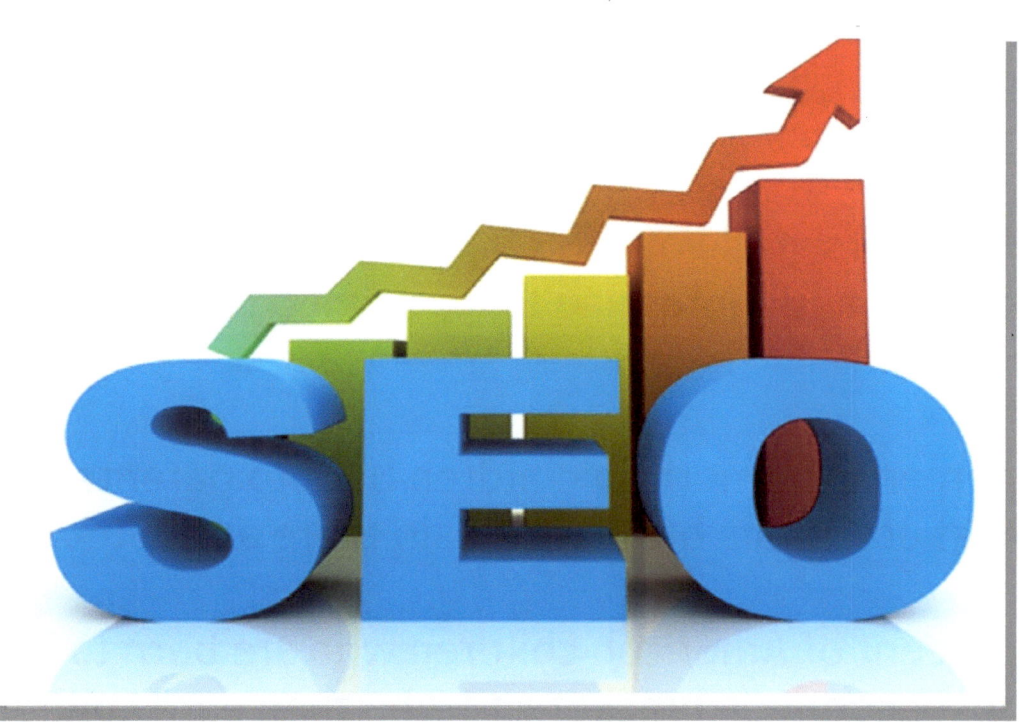

THE BASICS

Summerfest 2015 Festival Logo WHERE:Milwaukee, WI
WHEN:June 24-July 5, 2015
TICKETS: $19
CAMPING: No
WEBSITE: Official Website
THE SCENE

The World's Largest Music Festival hosts over 800 acts and 1,000 performances on 11 stages across 11 days in Milwaukee, WI.

THE BASICS

High Sierra Music Festival 2015 Festival Logo WHERE:Quincy, CA
WHEN:July 2-July 5, 2015
TICKETS: $260.50
CAMPING: Yes
WEBSITE: Official Website

Glendale Summer Band Concert Series
July 2 through July 23
Murphy Park
Glendale

The World of Entertainment

TOP PICKS OF THIS MONTH.....

**Encounters at the Heart of the World: A History of the Mandan People**
_**by**_
**Elizabeth A. Fenn**
**Winner of the 2015 Pulitzer Prize for History**

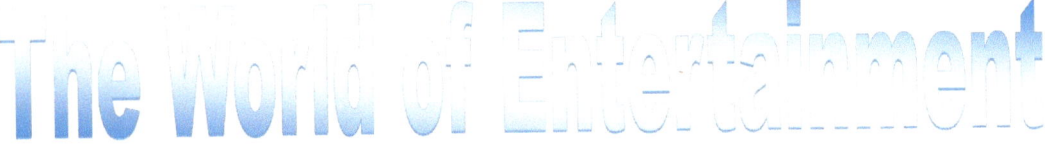

**Encounters at the Heart of the World concerns the Mandan Indians, iconic Plains people whose teeming, busy towns on the upper Missouri River were for centuries at the center of the North American universe.**

**The Pope and Mussolini: The Secret History of Pius XI and the Rise of Fascism in Europe**
_**by**_
**David I. Kertzer**
**PULITZER PRIZE WINNER**
**From National Book Award finalist David I. Kertz comes the gripping story of Pope Pius XI's secret relations with Italian dictator Benito Mussolini.**

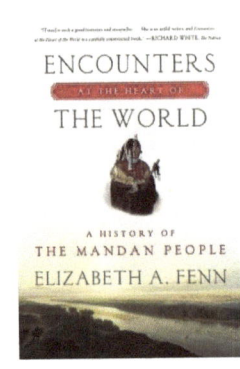

**The Wright Brothers**
**by David McCullough**
**Two-time winner of the Pulitzer Prize David McCullough tells the dramatic story-behind-the-story about the courageous brothers who taught the world how to fly:**

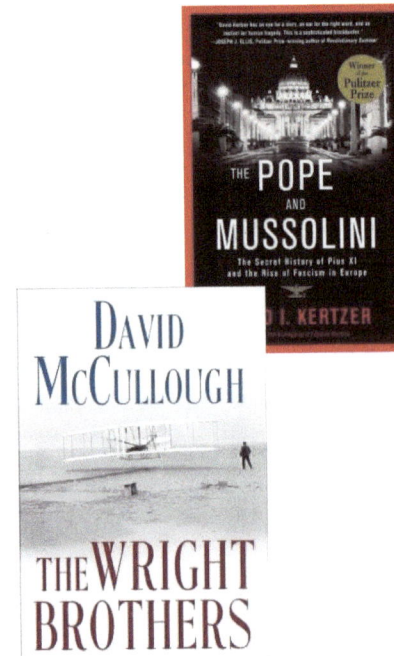

-

ENTERTAINMENT NIGHT LIFE

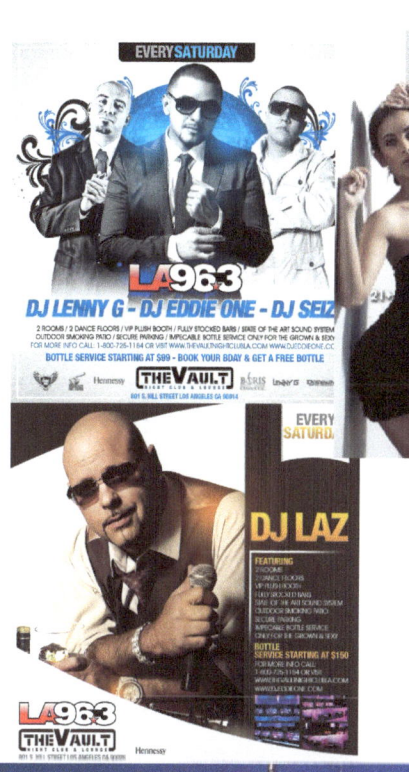

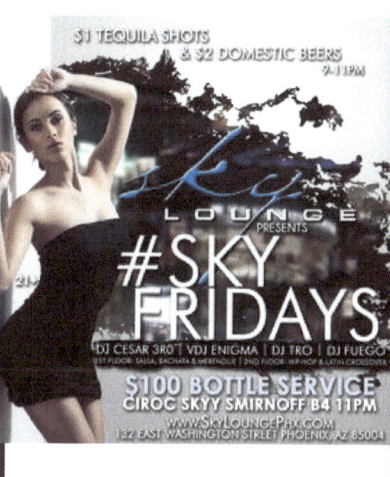

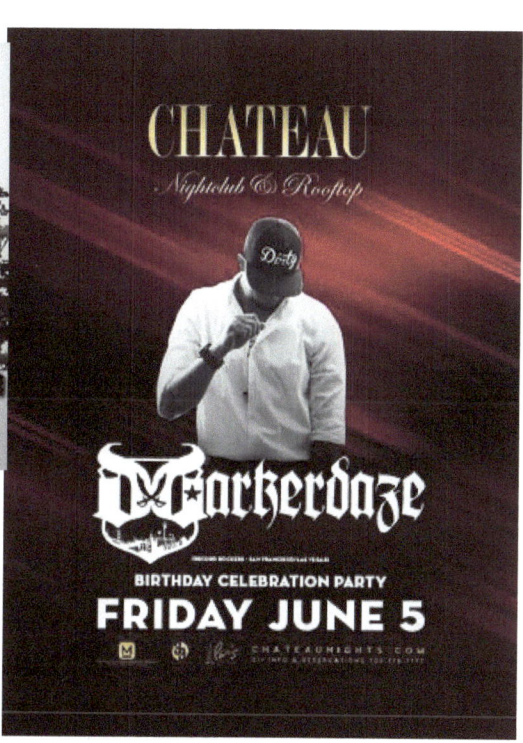

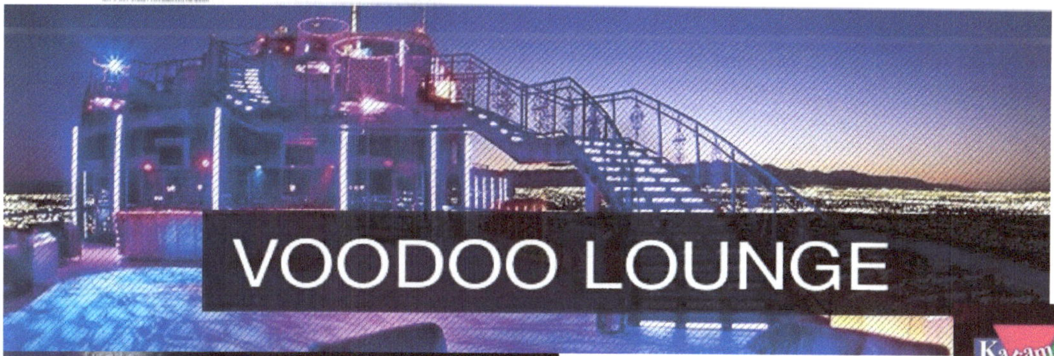

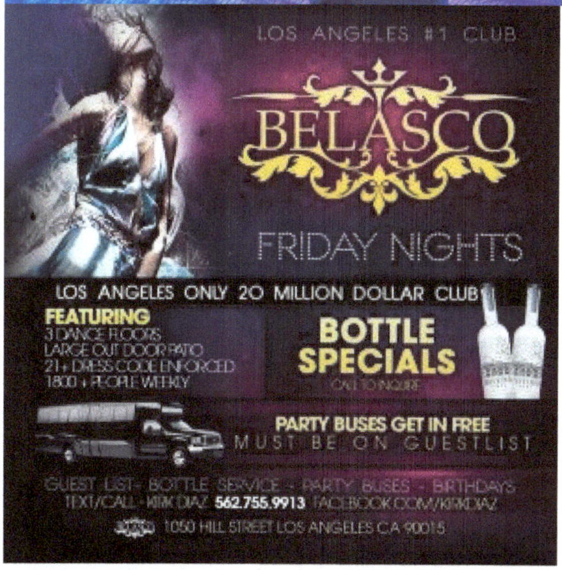

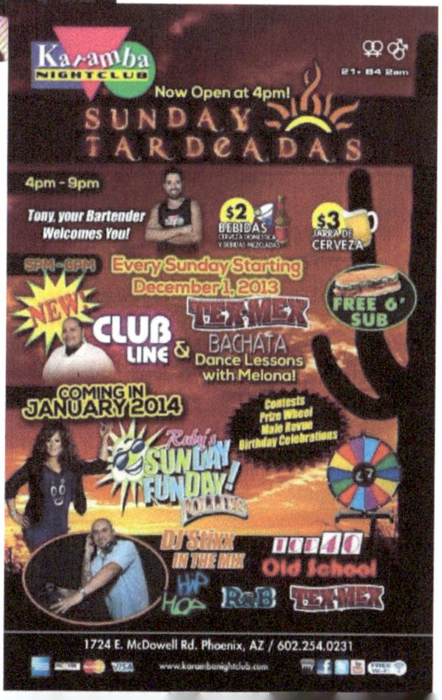

Workout Time: Getting Rid Of Those Love Handles

Love handles may sound (and feel) warm and delicious, but for most people, it's one of the hardest places to lose weight.

The term itself, used as a slang term to describe belly fat, wasn't popular until the 1960s when abdominal exercises began targeting these particular areas, says personal fitness trainer Kyla Gagnon of Inside Out Fitness based in Victoria, B.C.

Love handles are deposits of excess body fat that sit around your abdominal area, and most of us can pinch our belly fat from the front, back and sides. And it's not just about fitting into that dress or your favourite pair of jeans — excessive fat can also hurt your health. According to an article by Robert Glatter for Forbes, where you store your fat may increase your risk of developing diabetes or heart disease. Another study showed that larger BMIs increased the risk of obesity, according to Statistics Canada.

But physically losing those love handles won't actually get rid of any fat.

"Working the area with exercises will not get rid of the excess fat. What it will do is strengthen the muscles underneath the fat, which is important," Gagnon tells The Huffington Post Canada.

Instead, Gagnon says strengthening these areas and burning fats starts with the food on your plate. Avoid sugars, salts and unhealthy fats, and add fresh fruits, vegetables, good fats (like raw seeds or avocado) and lean clean proteins to your diet instead. Nutritionist Joy Bauer says that most diets are 90 per cent nutrition and 10 per cent exercise (or 10 per cent fun foods, as Bauer would say).

Ready to get started? Remember, always go at your own pace and incorporate weights only when you are comfortable.

Find out more by clicking on:

http://www.huffingtonpost.ca/2012/12/06/best-exercises-for-love-handles_n_2246243.html

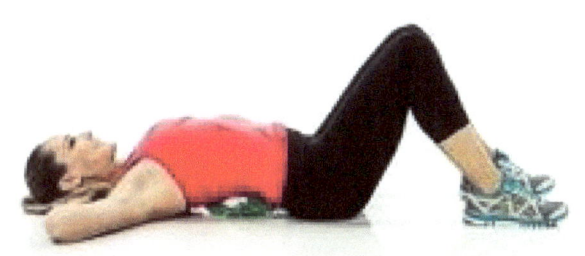
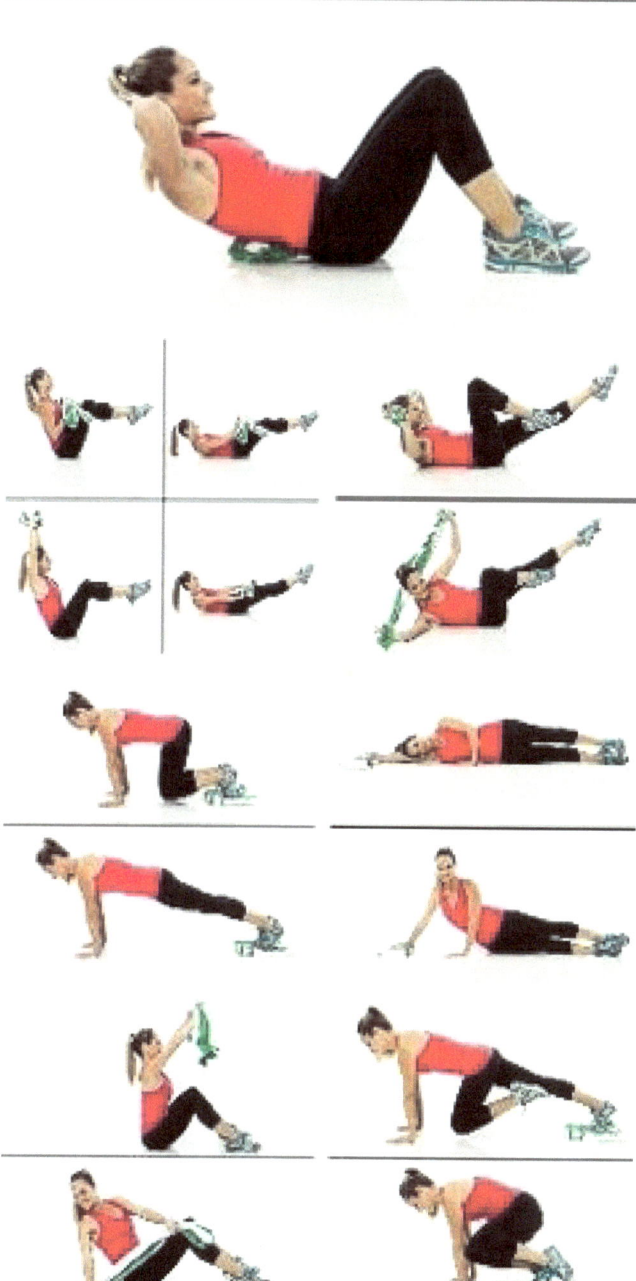

Fashion No or not....
Brought to you by: Lisabeths Design

Lisabeth Fashion Magazine

Pantone's- 2015 Newest Colors For Fashion

Get ready to wear lots and lots of purple next year: Pantone, the global authority on all things hue-related, has just announced Radiant Orchid as 2014's Color of the Year.

To come up with this particular shade, Pantone's team scoured the worlds of art, entertainment, fashion, travel and even sports to determine the most influential colors in each respective industry. In case you've forgotten, Emerald was 2013's Color of the Year; in 2012, it was Tangerine Tango.

So why Radiant Orchid for 2014? "While the 2013 color of the year, PANTONE 17-5641 Emerald, served as a symbol of growth, renewal and prosperity, Radiant Orchid reaches across the color wheel to intrigue the eye and spark the imagination," explains Leatrice Eiseman, executive director of the Pantone Color Institute, in this morning's release. "An enchanting harmony of fuchsia, purple and pink undertones, Radiant Orchid inspires confidence and emanates great joy, love and health. It is a captivating purple, one that draws you in with its beguiling charm." Sounds good to us.

From a fashion standpoint, we can totally see what inspired Pantone's pick; pale, vibrant purples were all over the Spring 2014 runways at Prabal Gurung, Missoni, Burberry Prorsum and Chanel, to name just a few. And beauty-wise, we think Radiant Orchid's a great choice: just think of all those bold lip colors to come.

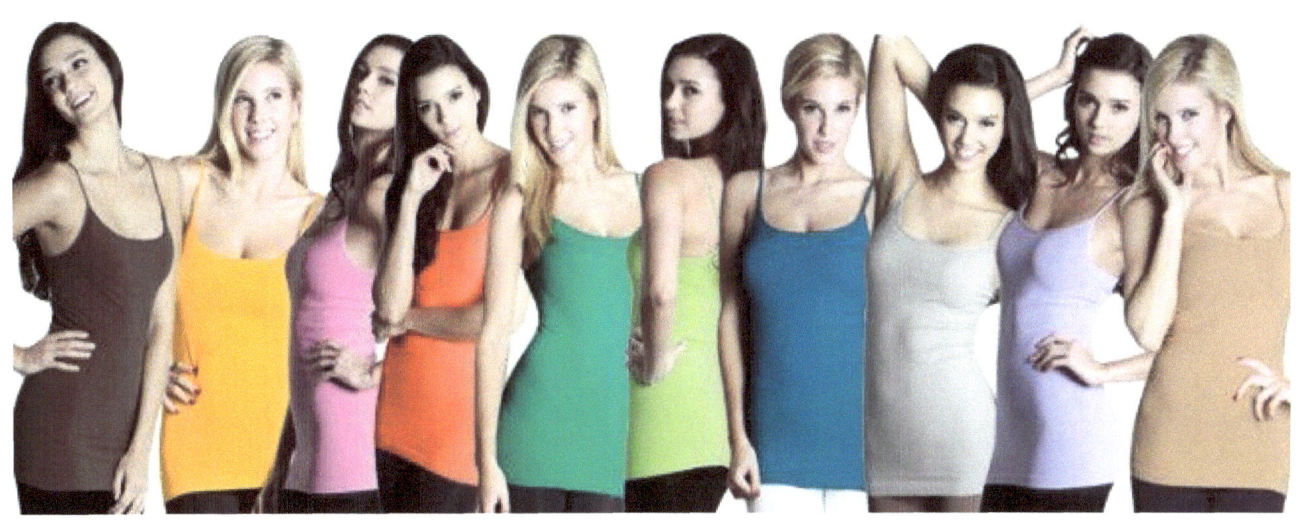

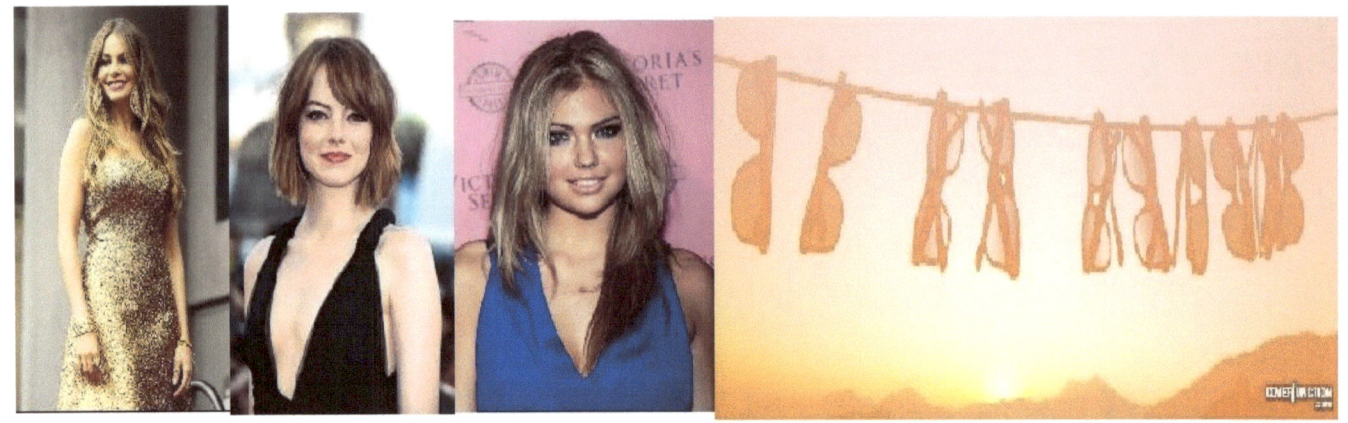

16 of July's Most Sizzling Summers Hotties Ladies Edition

Its a mans world but for our Julys Issue we decided to honor the women of our summers sizzling choice. Over music sports acting modeling etc, we think there is beauty in everything.

So our researchers found some inspiring ideas from other idealist who might have a word or two on beauty.

Beautiful. It's a powerful word, one not thrown around as frivolously as hot, pretty or any of the hundreds of words we've come to describe women, debasing their worth to nothing more than the symmetry of their face and the fullness of their lips.

It's a word that holds power and prestige far beyond that of any other adjective. It's a sacred word, one kept for those who truly can't be described any other way.

So with that being said here is our choice of *16 Of July's Most Sizzling Summers hotties Ladies Edition*

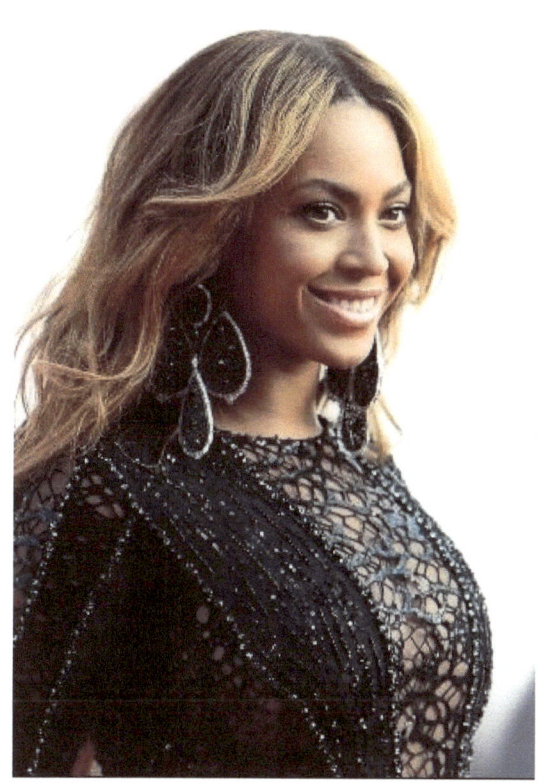

16). Beyoncé Giselle Knowles-Carter
Born September 4, 1981 (age 33)

is an American singer, songwriter, and actress. Born and raised in Houston, Texas, she performed in various singing and dancing competitions as a child, and rose to fame in the late 1990s as lead singer of R&B girl-group Destiny's Child. Managed by her father Mathew Knowles, the group became one of the world's best-selling girl groups of all time. Their hiatus saw the release of Beyoncé's debut album, Dangerously in Love (2003), which established her as a solo artist worldwide; it sold 11 million copies, earned five Grammy Awards and featured the Billboard Hot 100 number-one singles "Crazy in Love" and "Baby Boy".

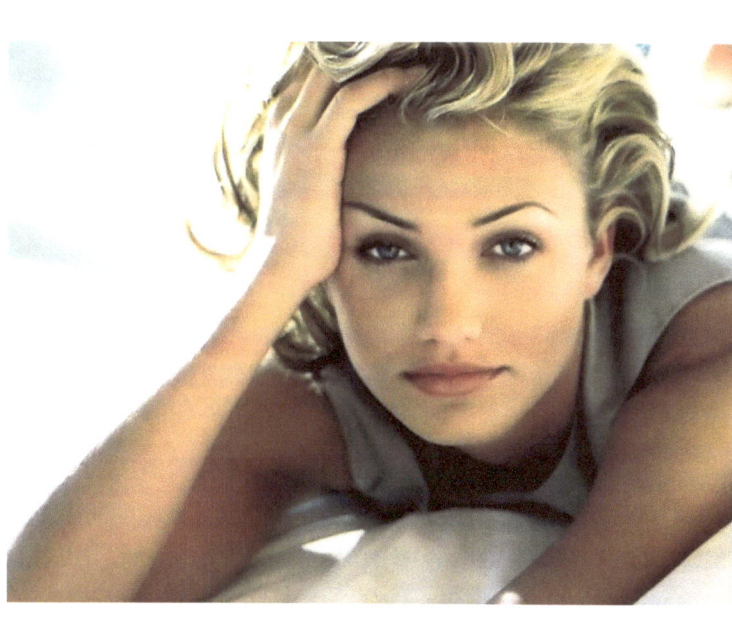

15.)Cameron Michelle Diaz
Born August 30, 1972
is an American actress, producer, and former fashion model. She rose to stardom in the 1990s with roles in The Mask (1994), My Best Friend's Wedding (1997) and There's Something About Mary (1998), and is also known for voicing the character of Princess Fiona in the Shrek series (2001–10). Other high-profile credits include Charlie's Angels (2000) and its sequel Charlie's Angels: Full Throttle (2003), The Holiday (2006), Knight and Day (2010), The Green Hornet (2011), Bad Teacher (2011), and The Other Woman (2014).

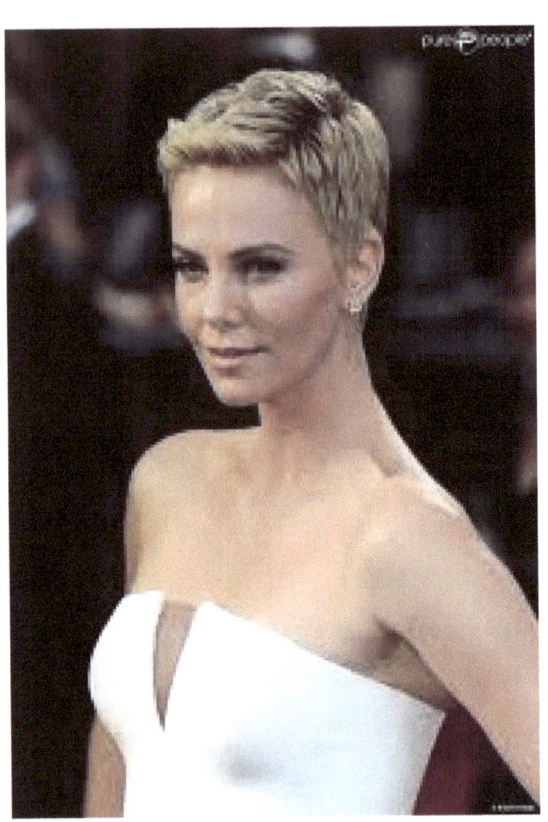

14.)Charlize Theron
Born August 7, 1975
is a South African and American actress, producer and fashion model. She has starred in several Hollywood films, such as The Devil's Advocate (1997), Mighty Joe Young (1998), The Cider House Rules (1999) and Mad Max: Fury Road (2015).
Theron received critical acclaim for her portrayal of serial killer Aileen Wuornos in Monster (2003), for which she won the Academy Award, Silver Bear, Golden Globe Award and Screen Actors Guild Award for Best Actress among several other accolades, becoming the first South African to win an Academy Award in a major acting category.

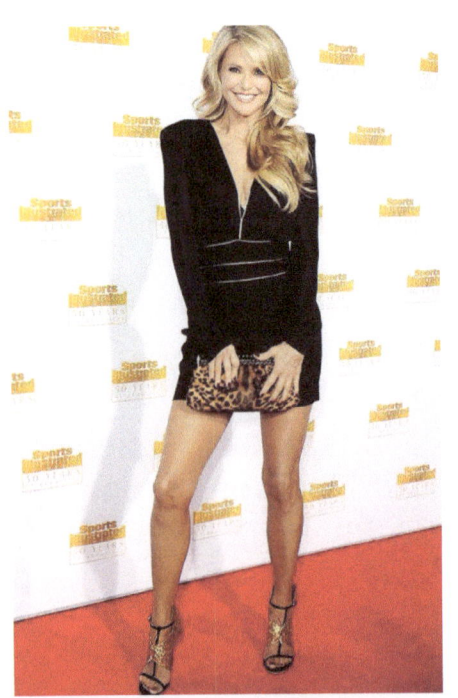

13.) Christie Brinkley
Born February 2, 1954
is an American model and actress. Brinkley gained worldwide fame beginning in the late 1970's with three consecutive Sports Illustrated Swimsuit Issue covers through 1981. She spent twenty five years as the face of CoverGirl (the longest running cosmetics contract of any model in history), has appeared on over 500 magazine covers, and has signed contracts with major brands—both fashion and non-fashion.

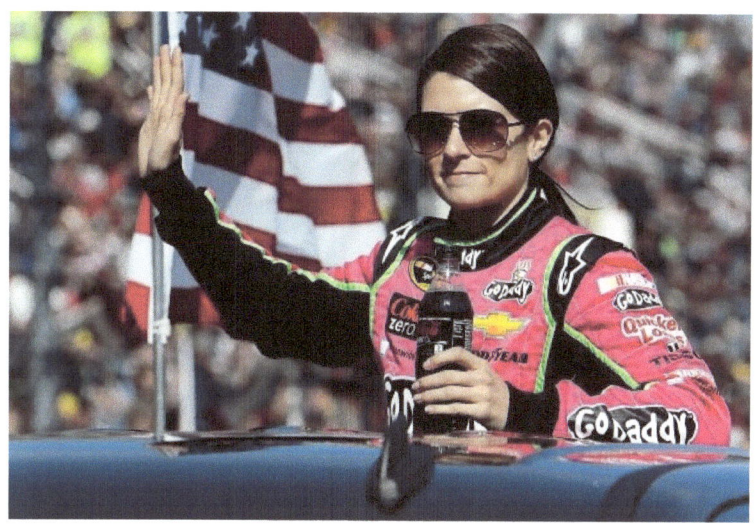

12.) Danica Sue Patrick
Born March 25, 1982 (age 33)

is an American auto racing driver, model, and advertising spokeswoman. She is the most successful woman in the history of American open-wheel racing—her win in the 2008 Indy Japan 300 is the only women's victory in an IndyCar Series race and her third place in the 2009 Indianapolis 500 the highest finish there ever by a woman. She competed in the series from 2005 to 2011. In 2012, she competed in the NASCAR Nationwide Series and occasionally in the NASCAR Sprint Cup Series. Since the 2013 season, Patrick has driven the #10 Chevrolet SS for Stewart-Haas Racing in the Sprint Cup Series.

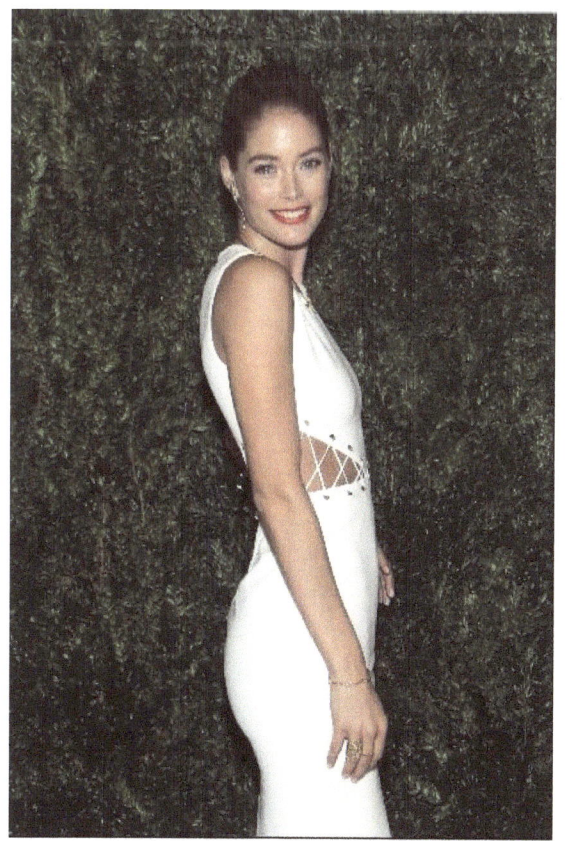

11.) Doutzen Kroes
Born Jaury 23, 1985 30 years old

is a Dutch model and actress and former Victoria's Secret Angel. She started working for the brand in 2004, becoming an Angel in 2008 and finally leaving the brand in 2015. She is on contract with L'Oréal. In 2014, Kroes came in second on the Forbes top-earning models list (after Gisele Bündchen), estimated to have earned $8 million in one year

10.)Emily Jean "Emma" Stone
born November 6, 1988

is an American actress. She made her feature film debut in the comedy Superbad (2007). She co-starred in the comedies The House Bunny (2008), Zombieland (2009), and Paper Man (2009). In 2010, Stone made her leading debut in the comedy Easy A, for which she received a nomination for the Golden Globe Award for Best Actress – Musical or Comedy. Stone's other films include the romantic comedy-drama Crazy, Stupid, Love (2011), the drama The Help (2011), The Amazing Spider-Man film series (2012, 2014) as Gwen Stacy and the animated comedy The Croods (2013).

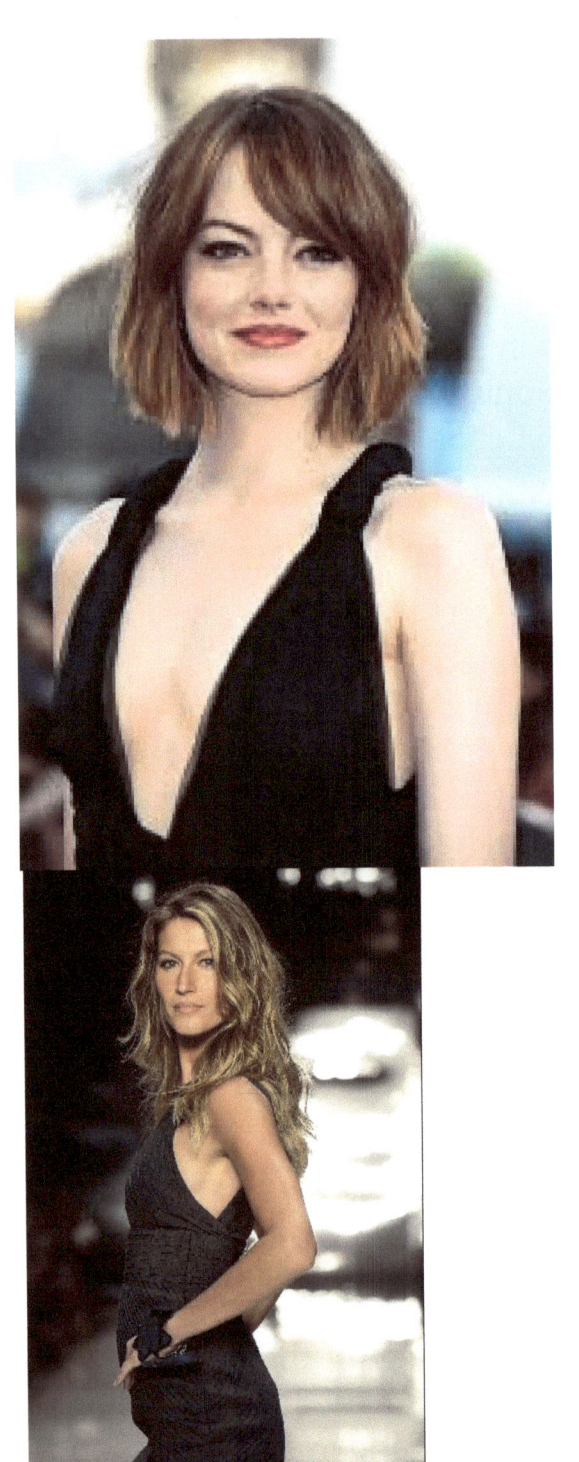

9.Gisele Caroline Bündchen
Born July 20, 1980
is a Brazilian fashion model, actress, and producer. She is the Goodwill Ambassador for the United Nations Environment Programme.[7]
In the late 1990s, Bündchen was the first in a wave of Brazilian models to find international success.[8] In 1999, Vogue noted "The Return of the Sexy Model", and she was credited with ending the "heroin chic" era of modeling. Bündchen was one of the Victoria's Secret Angels from 2000 until mid-2007. Bündchen pioneered the "horse walk", a stomping movement created when a model picks her knees up high and kicks her feet out in front.[9] Claudia Schiffer and Naomi Campbell have stated that Bündchen is the only remaining true supermodel.[10]

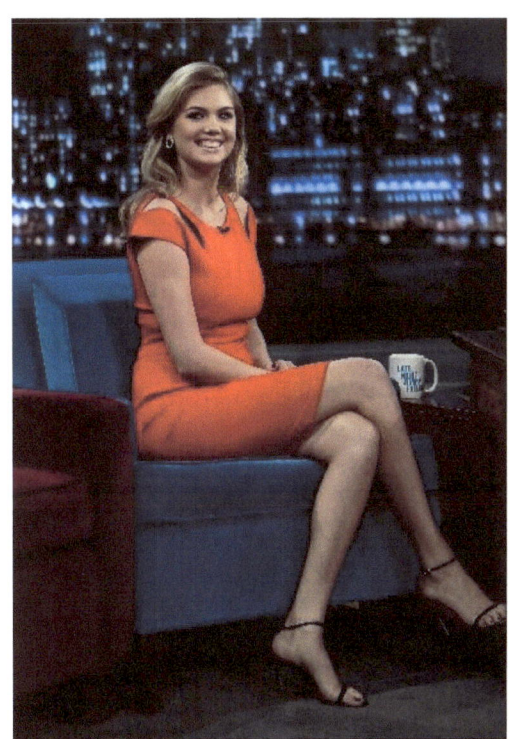

8) Katherine Elizabeth "Kate" Upton born June 10, 1992
is an American model and actress, known for her appearances in the Sports Illustrated Swimsuit Issue.[7] Upton was named Rookie of the Year following her first appearance in 2011[7] and was the cover model for the 2012 and 2013 issues.[8] She was also the subject of the 100th anniversary Vanity Fair cover. Upton has also appeared in the financially successful films Tower Heist (2011) and The Other Woman (2014).

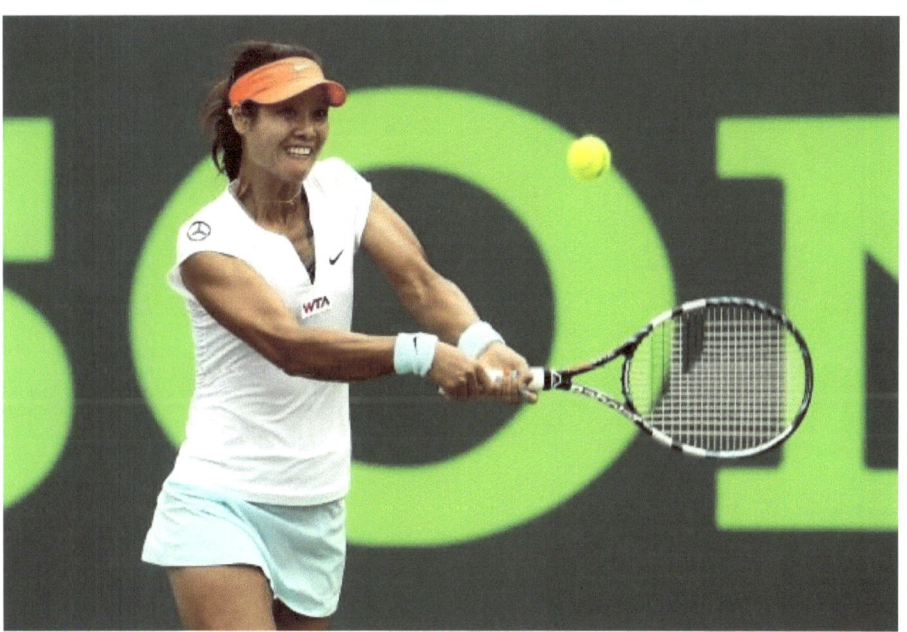

7.) Li Na
Born February 26 1982
is a Chinese former professional tennis player, who achieved a career-high ranking of world No. 2 on the WTA Tour on 17 February 2014, but retired from the sport seven months later due to a chronic left knee injury that had kept her out of the game for many years previously. Over the course of her career, Li won nine WTA singles titles, including two Grand Slam singles titles at the 2011 French Open and 2014 Australian Open.

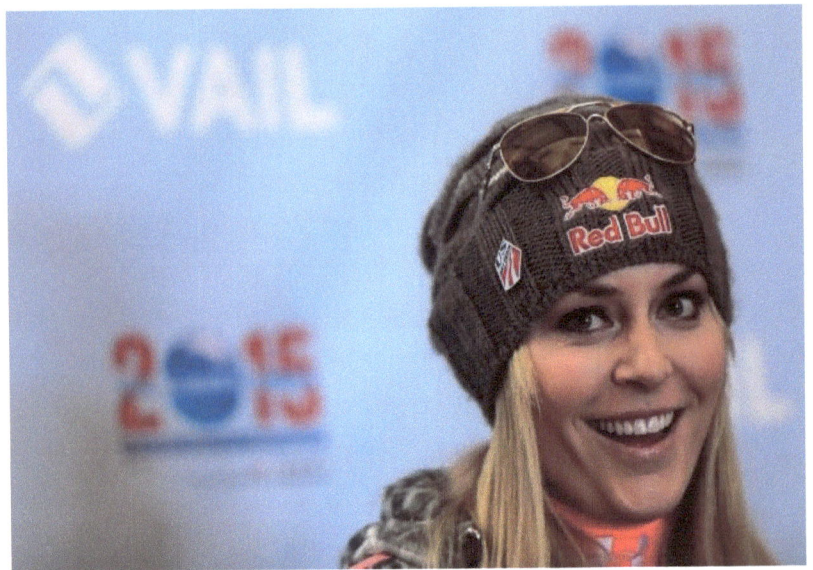

6.) Lindsey Vonn
Born October 18, 1984

is an American World Cup alpine ski racer on the US Ski Team. She has won four World Cup championships—one of two female skiers to do so, along with Annemarie Moser-Pröll—with three consecutive titles in 2008, 2009 and 2010,[2] plus another in 2012.[3] Vonn won the gold medal in downhill at the 2010 Winter Olympics, the first ever in the event for an American woman

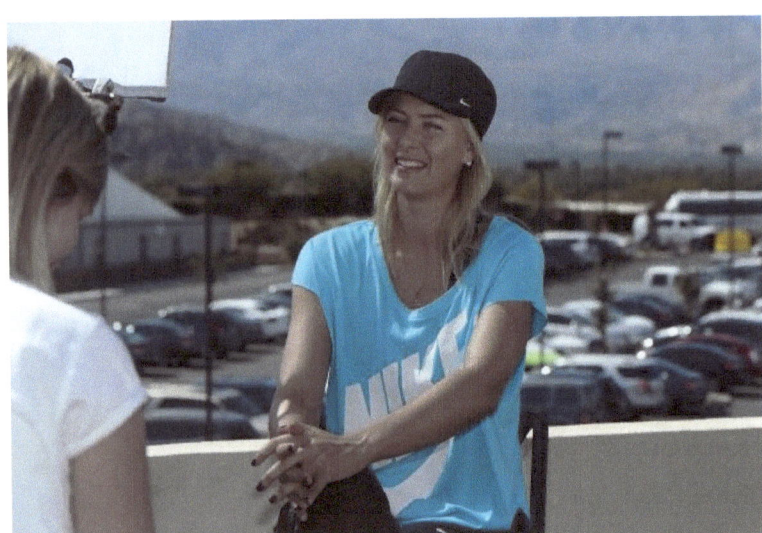

5.) Maria Sharapova
Born April 19, 1987

is a Russian professional tennis player, who is ranked world No. 4 by the Women's Tennis Association (WTA). A United States resident since 1994,[4] Sharapova has competed on the WTA tour since 2001. She has been ranked world No. 1 in singles by the WTA on five separate occasions, for a total of 21 weeks. She is one of ten women, and the lone Russian, to hold the career Grand Slam and is an Olympic medalist, having earned silver for Russia in women's singles at the 2012 Summer Olympics in London.

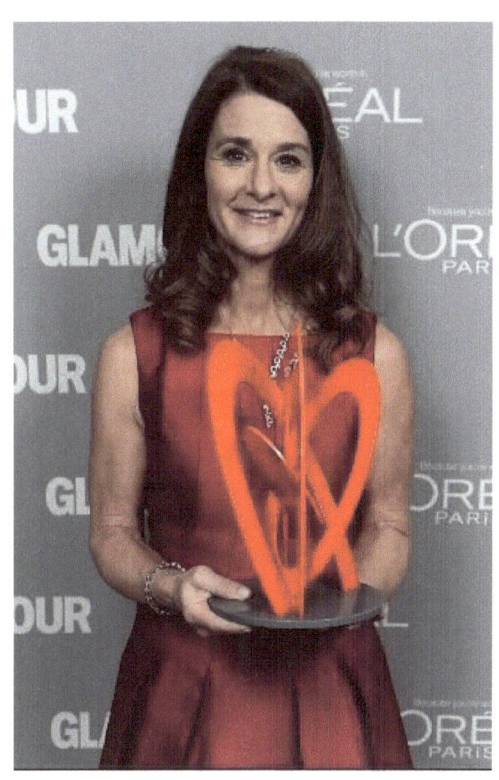

4.) Melinda Gates
Born August 15, 1964

is an American businessperson and philanthropist. She is the wife of Bill Gates, and the co-founder of the Bill & Melinda Gates Foundation.

3.) Oprah Winfrey
Born January 29, 1954

is an American media proprietor, talk show host, actress, producer, and philanthropist.[1] Winfrey is best known for her talk show The Oprah Winfrey Show, which was the highest-rated program of its kind in history and was nationally syndicated from 1986 to 2011.[5] Dubbed the "Queen of All Media",[6] she has been ranked the richest African-American of the 20th century

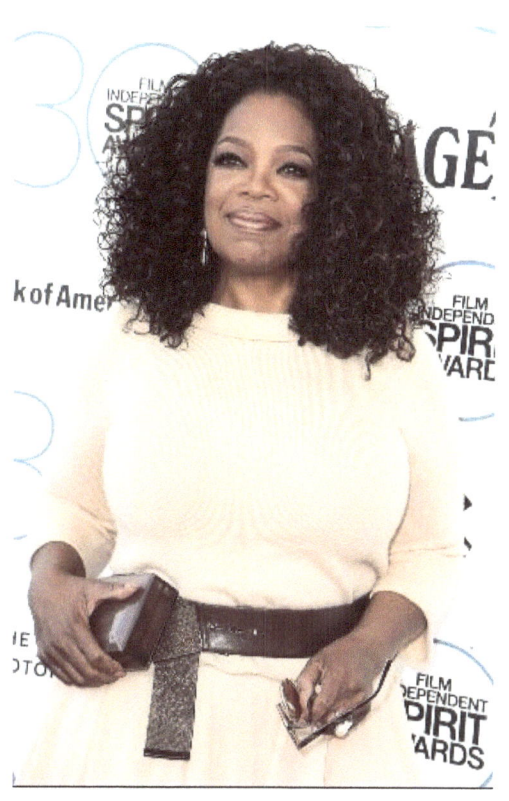

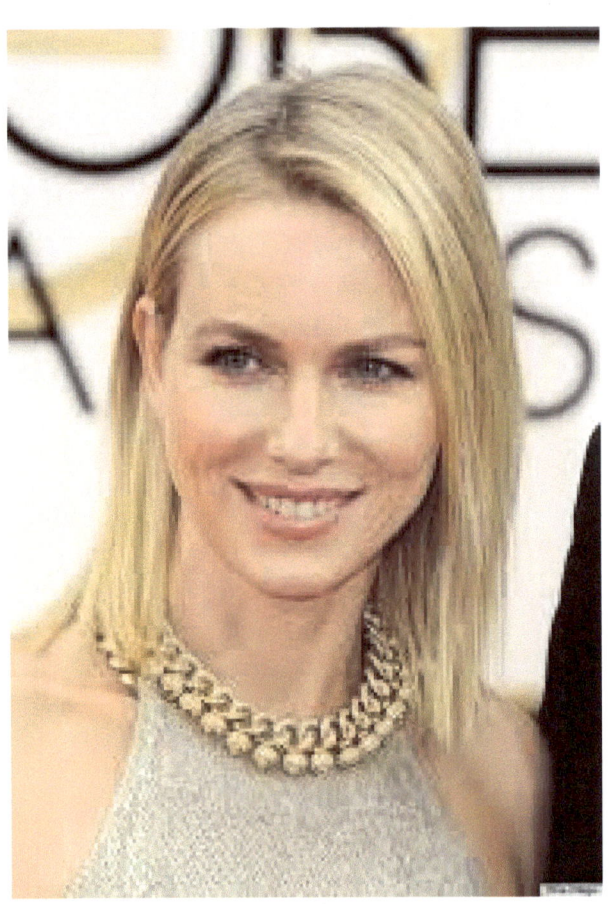

2.) Naomi Watts
Born September 28, 1968

is a British actress. She made her screen debut in the Australian drama film For Love Alone (1986) and then appeared in the television series Hey Dad..! (1990), Brides of Christ (1991) and Home and Away (1991) and alongside Nicole Kidman and Thandie Newton in the coming-of-age comedy-drama film Flirting (1991). After moving to America, Watts appeared in films, including Tank Girl (1995), Children of the Corn IV: The Gathering (1996) and Dangerous Beauty (1998) and had the lead role in the television series Sleepwalkers

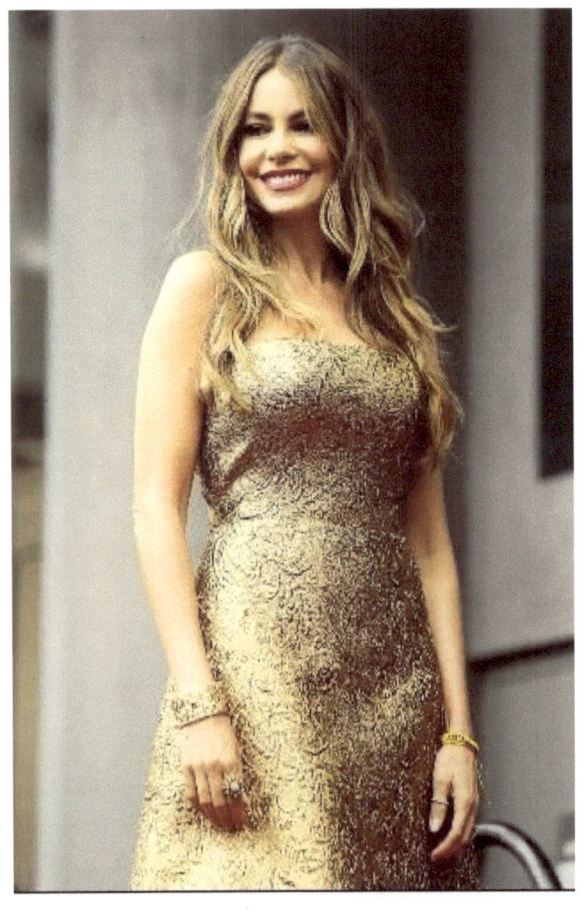

1.) Sofia Vergara
Born July 10, 1972

is a Colombian-American actress, comedian, producer, television host, model and businesswoman.
Vergara was widely known for co-hosting two television shows for Spanish-language television network Univisión in the late 1990s. Her first notable acting job in English was in the film Chasing Papi (2003). Subsequently, she appeared in other films, including Four Brothers (2005) and two Tyler Perry films—Meet the Browns (2008) and Madea Goes to Jail (2009), receiving an ALMA Award nomination for the latter. Vergara's success on television has earned her roles in recent films The Smurfs (2011), New Year's Eve (2011), Happy Feet Two (2011), The Three Stooges (2012), Escape from Planet Earth (2013), Machete Kills (2013), Chef (2014), and Hot Pursuit (2015). In 2012 and 2013, she was the top-earning actress on US television

Trendy News What You Want To Know

Watch: Steve Harvey shakes it with 'DWTS' pro Karina Smirnoff on 'Celebrity Family Feud'

Survey says Steve Harvey has moves like Jagger!

The host took a turn on the game show floor with Dancing With the Stars pro Karina Smirnoff on Sunday after the leggy lady in red asked him about his "amazing moves."

Which confused Harvey because your mind basically lives and gets mail in the gutter when you work on a show like Family Feud.

-

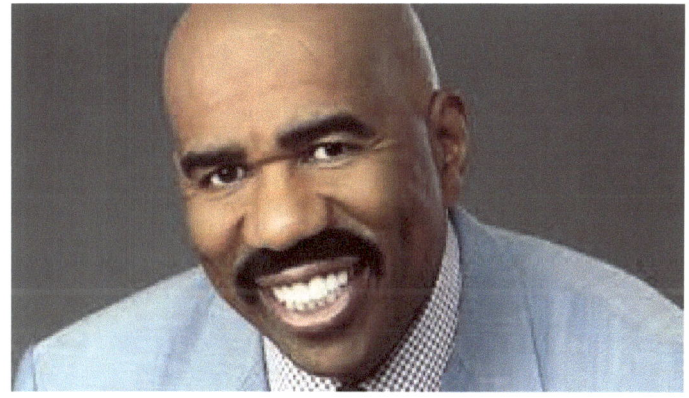

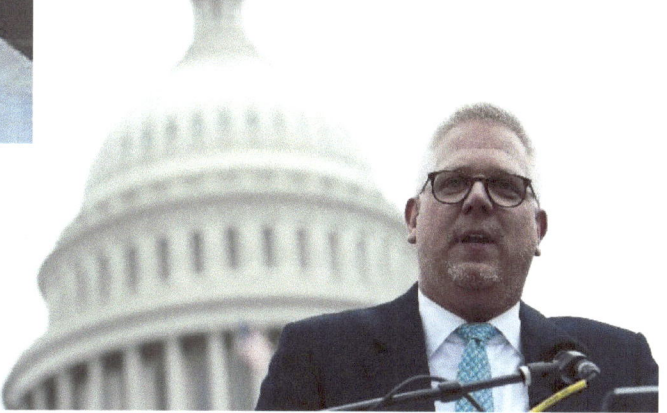

No, Glenn Beck Isn't On The 2015 Celebrity 100--But He Is Worth More Than $100 Million

Glenn Beck doesn't mince words. So neither will I. Beck, the conservative commentator who has pushed his popular and devotedly partisan shtick well beyond Fox News, is missing from the latest Celebrity 100.

Trendy News What You Want To Know

1-2 punch: Floyd Mayweather, Manny Pacquiao top Forbes celebrity earnings

Fresh off the heels of their May 2 clash, Floyd Mayweather and Manny Pacquiao topped the list of highest-paid celebrities in the world, as compiled by Forbes magazine from May 2014 through May 2015.

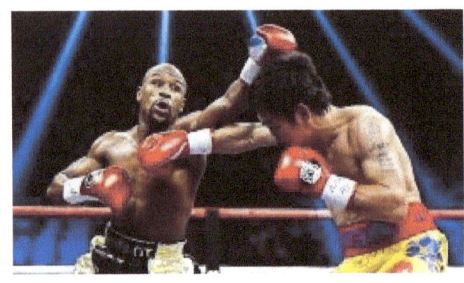

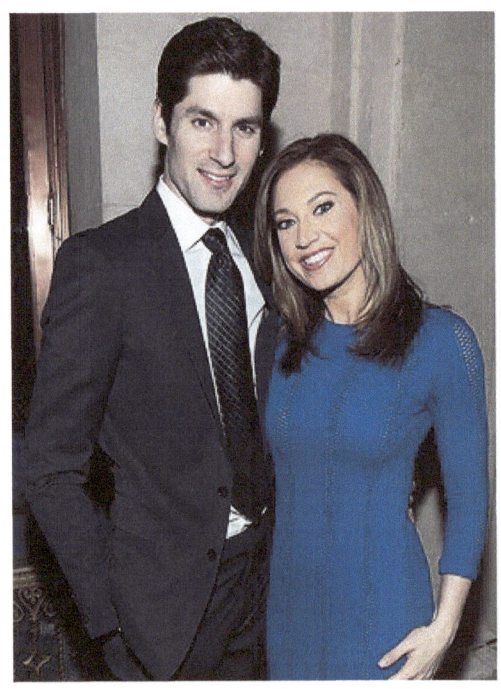

Ginger Zee Expecting First Child

Ginger Zee's future is looking bright: she's pregnant!

The ABC chief meteorologist is expecting her first child with husband Ben Aaron, she announced Monday on Good Morning America.

"This is the most nervous I've been in awhile," the mom-to-be says. "The forecast for delivery is in December."

Trendy News What You Want To Know

Celebrity Genealogy on TV: Who and When?

History and genealogy geeks are delighted with the TLC announcement that its popular celebrity roots series, Who Do You Think You Are? (WDYTYA), will be back for its seventh season starting on July 26. Stepping into the ancestral spotlight this time are Tom Bergeron, Bryan Cranston, Ginnifer Goodwin, and Alfre Woodard. And happily for millions of Harry Potter fans, an episode of the original U.K. series focusing on J.K. Rowling will also be adapted and incorporated into the lineup.

Who Do You Think You Are?: The Essential Guide to Tracing Your Family History Paperback

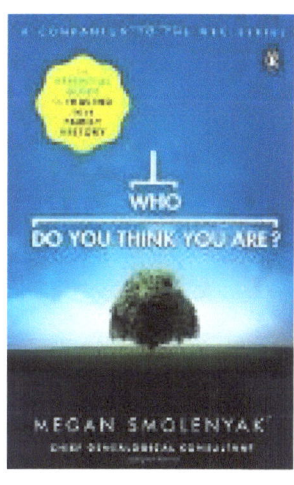

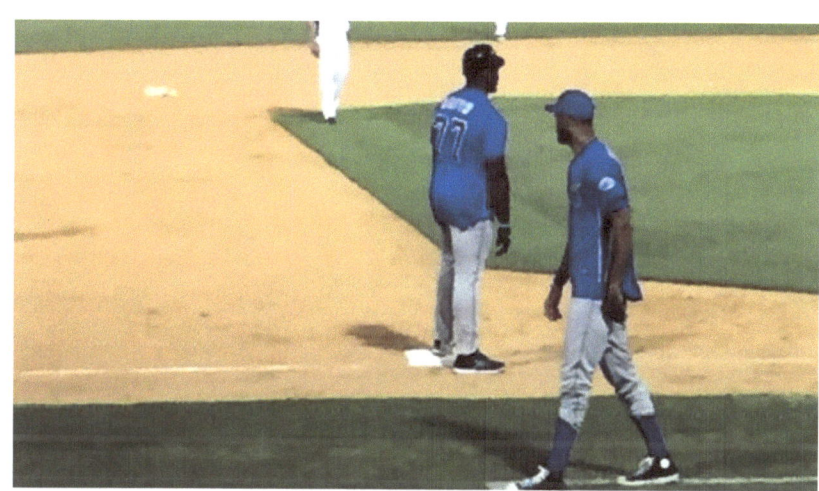

Tyron Smith: 2015 Dirk Nowitzki Heroes Celebrity Baseball Game MVP

Tyron Smith might be the best left tackle in football. He was definitely the best player in Dirk Nowitzki's Heroes Celebrity Baseball Game on Saturday night at Dr. Pepper Ballpark in Frisco.

Smith fell a home run short of the cycle and took home MVP honors for his three-hit performance for the Blue Sox, who won 17-5 over a White Sox team that featured Nowitzki, Steve Nash and Smith's Cowboys teammate Dez Bryant.

New Technology For The Modern Geek

Bondic
Liquid Plastic Welder

Speed of Light

We usually don't notice how many household items are tough to fix . . . until one breaks. A broken part, even if it's small, can render an entire device unusable. That makes too much of what we own,

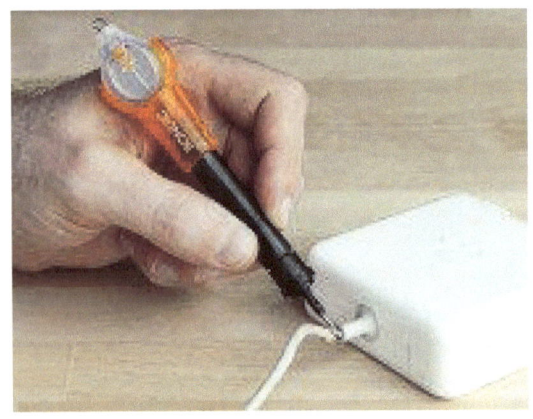

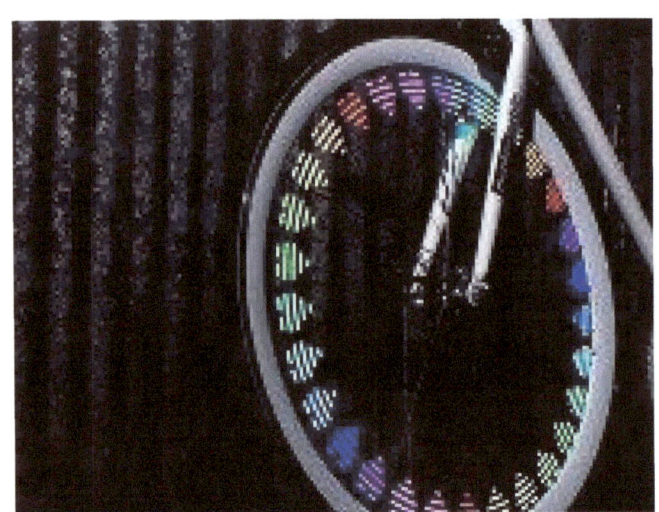

MonkeyLectric Monkey Lights

Bike Wheel Lights

Light the Night

When riding your bike at dusk or in the dark, it's important to make sure you can be seen. MonkeyLectric helps you stand out in style by digitally displaying bright, colorful lights and designs

New Technology For The Modern Geek

Smartphone Projector

Portable Video Projector

Simple Cinema

Turn on your phone and gather 'round. The Smartphone Projector turns any surface into your own private cinema.

Luckies of London makes this simple DIY projector out of sturdy cardboard and a glass

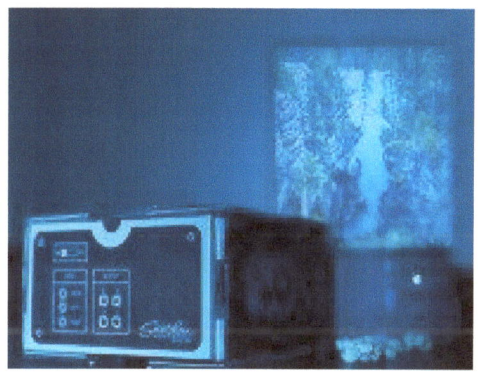 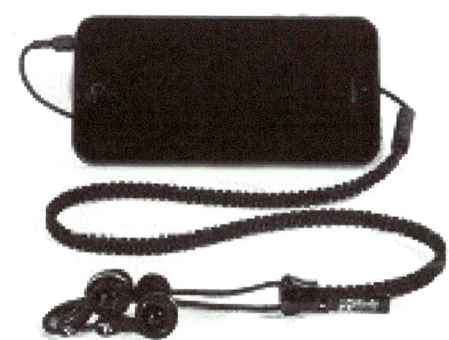

Zipbuds

Tangle-Free Earbuds

Tunes Without Tangles

Life gets messy, but your headphones don't need to be. These earbuds put an end to the perpetual problem of tangled headphone

New Technology VS The Other Guy

Samsung Unveils Tech That Can Double Lithium-Ion Battery Capacity

Battery life has been one of the biggest concerns for smartphone owners; though if a new study published in a journal last week is to be believed, then lithium-ion batteries might soon offer twice their capacity soon.

Published by researchers at Samsung, the study claims the new technology can enable batteries to offer up to 1.5 and 1.8 times higher capacity than those of current commercial lithium-ion batteries. Samsung has come up with new coating technique for battery cathodes that promises to overcome limitations of current lithium ion batteries.

As per the study, published in Nature Communications, the new battery technology that employs use of graphene on the silicon surface offers volume expansion that can give extended battery life.

As per the study, published in Nature Communications, the new battery technology that employs use of graphene on the silicon surface offers volume expansion that can give extended battery life.

The journal explains, "Here we report direct graphene growth over silicon nanoparticles without silicon carbide formation. The graphene layers anchored onto the silicon surface accommodate the volume expansion of silicon via a sliding process between adjacent graphene layers. When paired with a commercial lithium cobalt oxide cathode, the silicon carbide-free graphene coating allows the full cell to reach volumetric energy densities of 972 and 700 Wh l-1 at first and 200th cycle, respectively, 1.8 and 1.5 times higher than those of current commercial lithium-ion batteries."

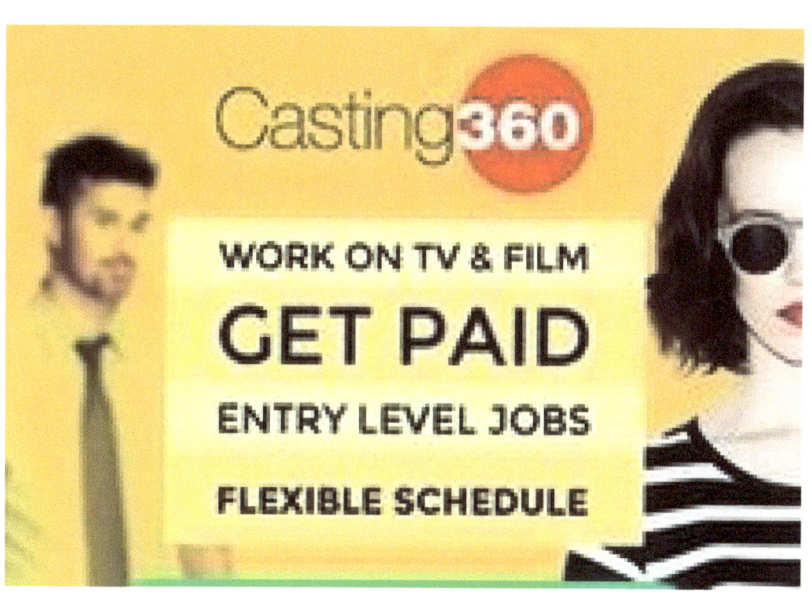

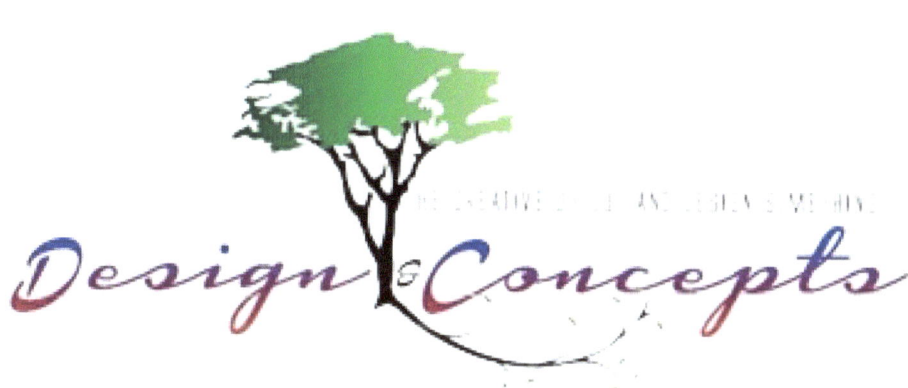

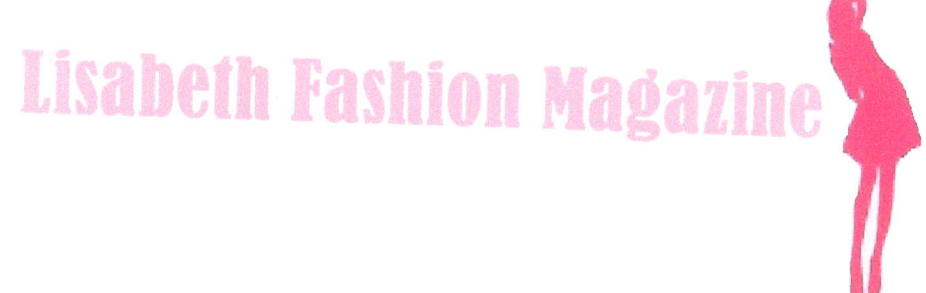

Social apps and more
Find us !

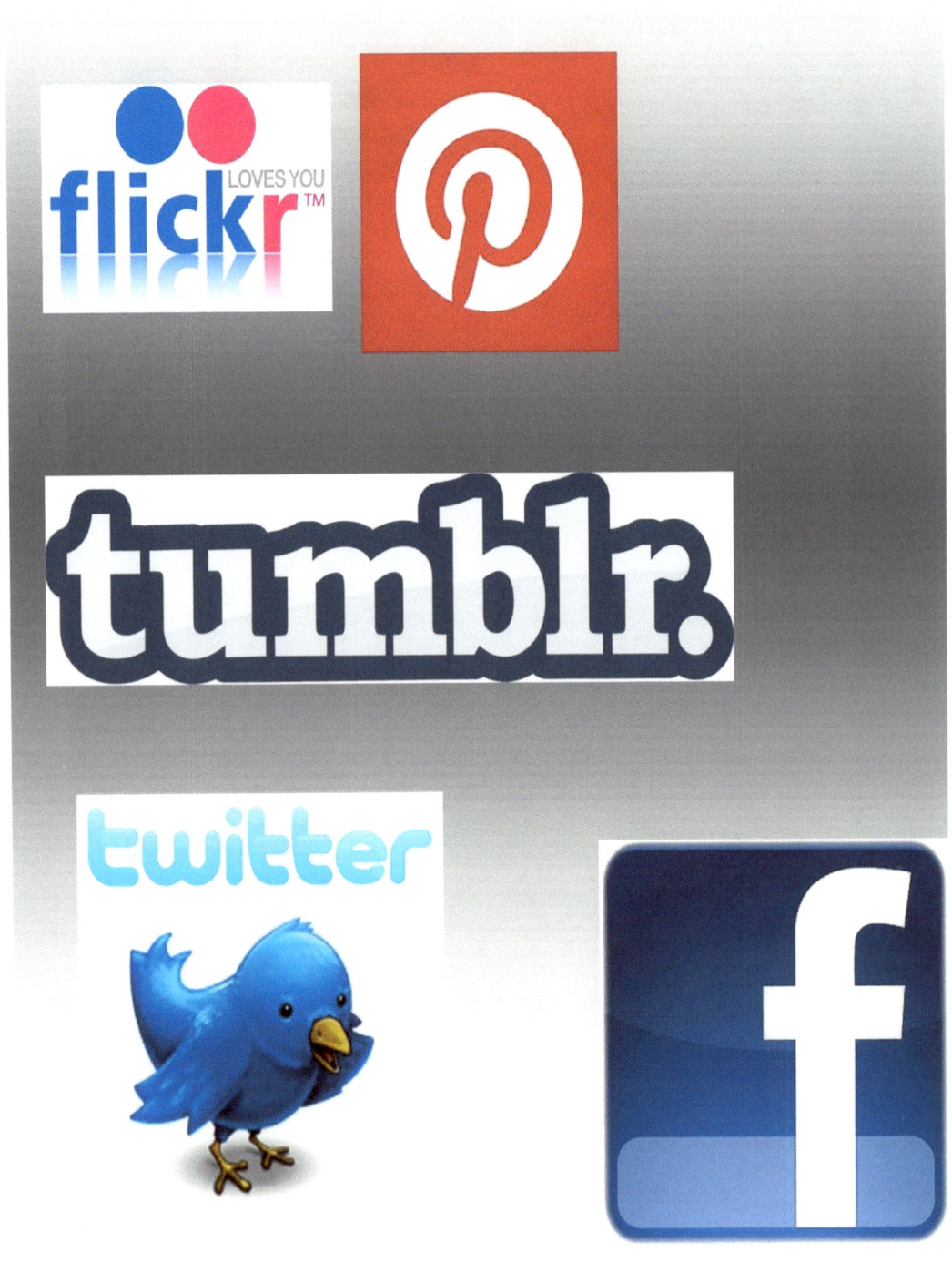

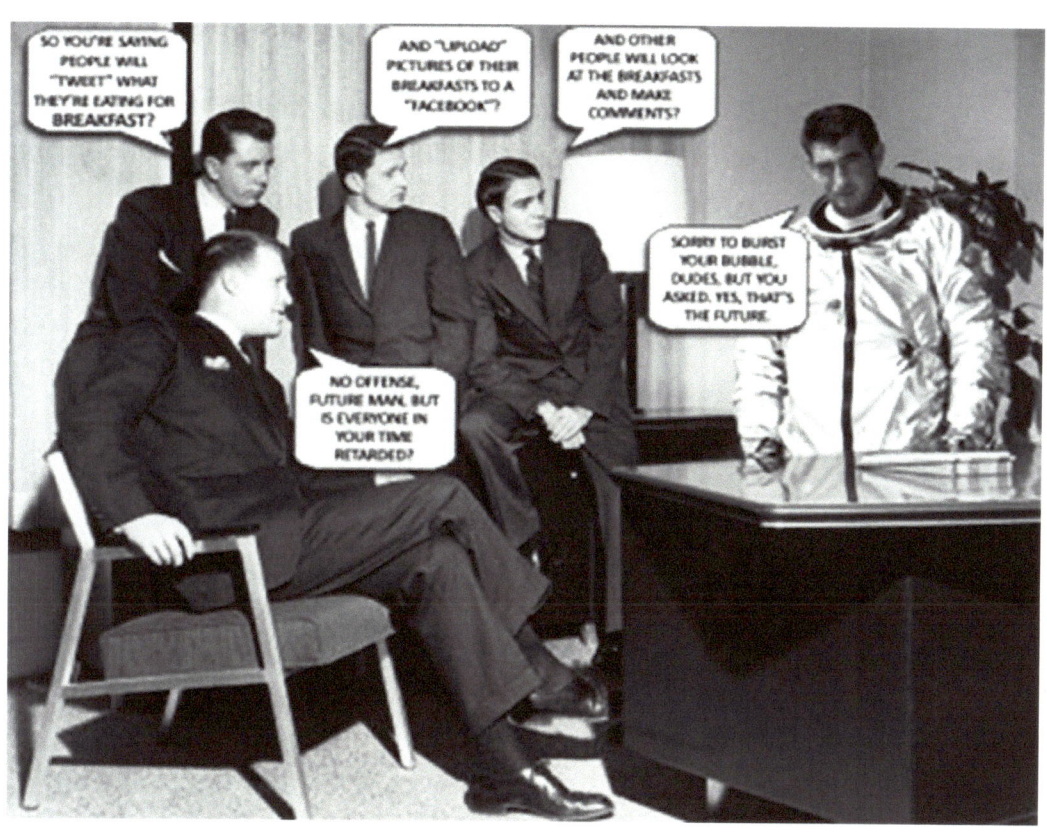

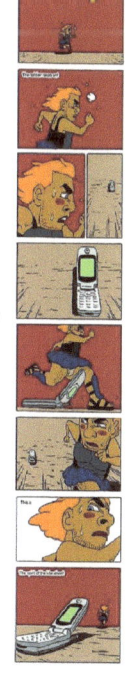

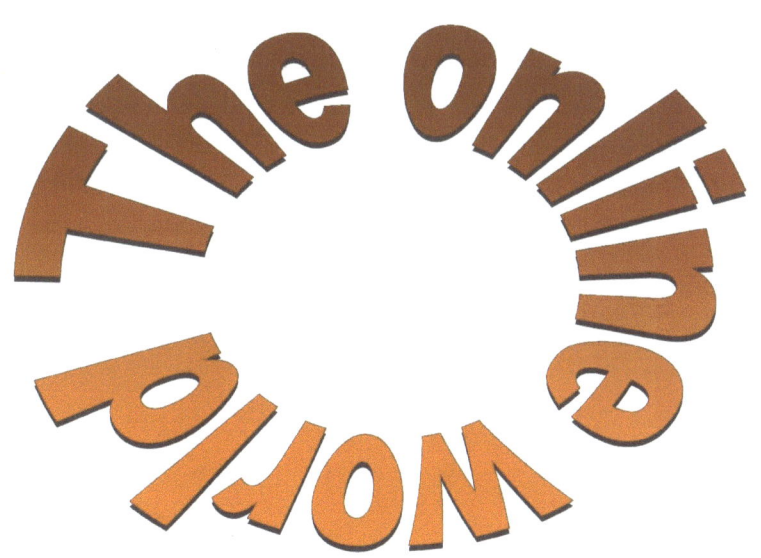

Home and Garden: 7 Secrets For A High-Yield Vegetable Garden

Imagine harvesting nearly half a ton of tasty, beautiful, organically grown vegetables from a 15-by-20-foot plot, 100 pounds of tomatoes from just 100 square feet (a 4-by-25-foot bed), or 20 pounds of carrots from just 24 square feet. Yields like these are easier to achieve than you may think. The secret to superproductive gardening is taking the time now to plan strategies that will work for your garden. Here are seven high-yield strategies gleaned from gardeners who have learned to make the most of their garden space.

1. Build Up Your Soil
 Expert gardeners agree that building up the soil is the single most important factor in pumping up yields.

2. Round Out Your Beds
 The shape of your beds can make a difference, too. Raised beds are more space-efficient if the tops are gently rounded to form an arc.

3. Space Smartly
 To get the maximum yields from each bed, pay attention to how you arrange your plants.

4. Grow Up
 No matter how small your garden, you can grow more by going vertical.

5. Mix It Up
 Interplanting compatible crops saves space, too. Consider the classic Native American combination, the "three sisters"—corn, beans, and squash.

6. Succeed With Successions
Succession planting allows you to grow more than one crop in a given space over the course of a growing season.

7. Stretch Your Season
 Adding a few weeks to each end of the growing season can buy you enough time to grow yet another succession crop—say a planting of leaf lettuce, kale, or turnips—or to harvest more end-of-the-season tomatoes.

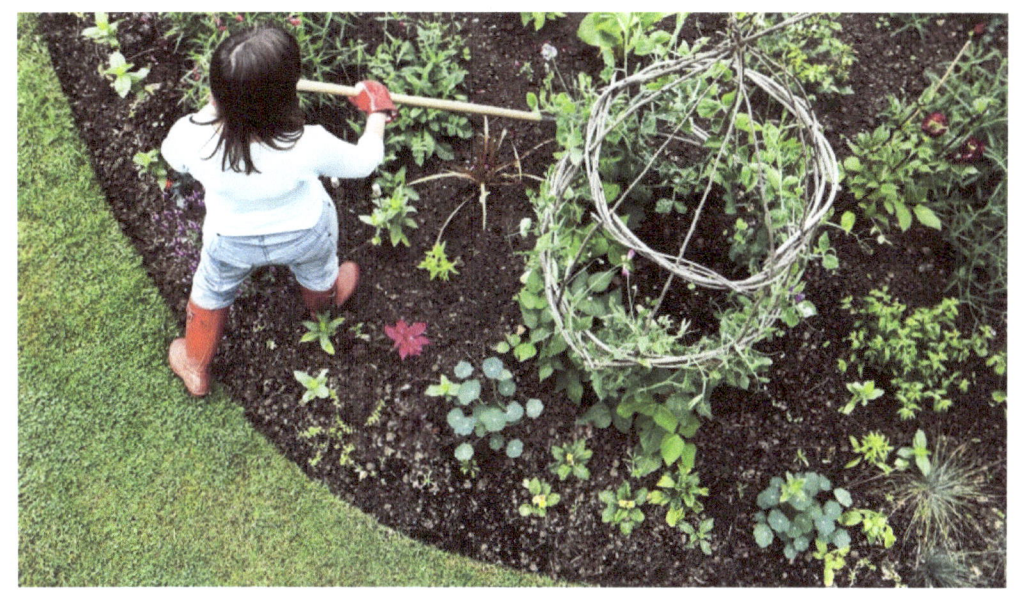

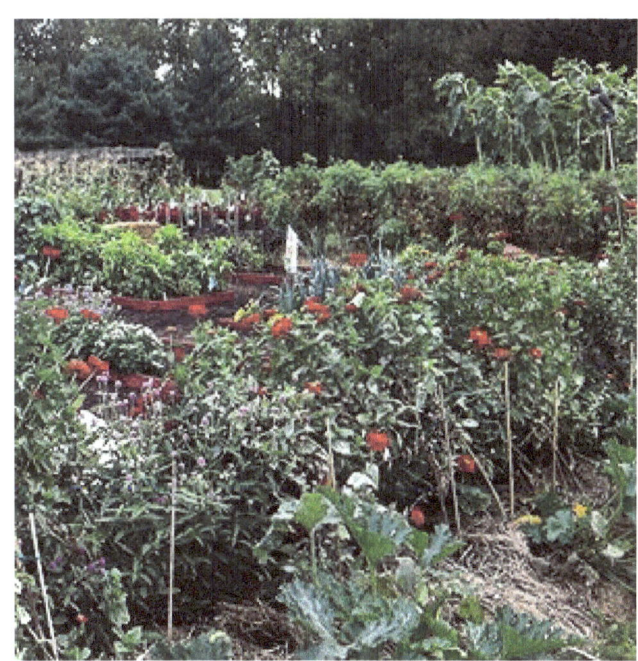

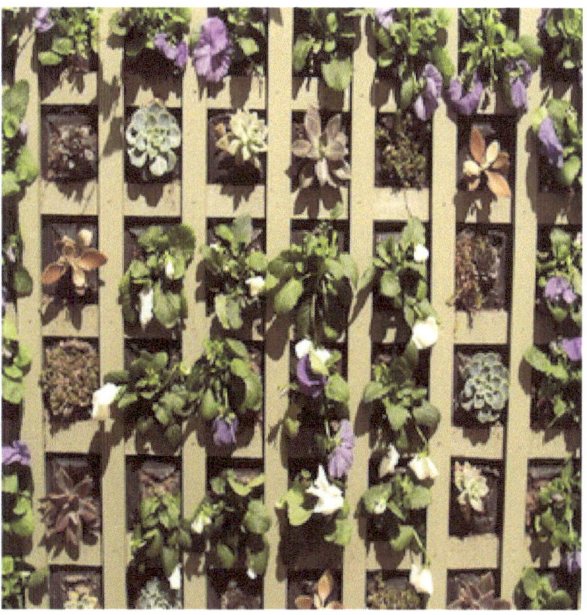

Before & After: The Hive That Could Revolutionize Beekeeping For

When my third-grade class studied a unit on honeybees, my dad, who learned beekeeping from his grandfather, agreed to give a presentation about his hobby. We giggled when he outfitted one of my friends in his bee suit—with the oversized veil and gigantic coveralls, she looked like a miniature spaceman.

Fast forward 17 years and you'll find a new technology that may result in fewer beekeepers looking like they just returned from the moon. Flow Hive, which recently raised more than $12 million on crowdfunding site Indiegogo, allows honey to be harvested via tap with the turn of a lever, leaving both bees and beekeepers theoretically undisturbed.

At first, I was skeptical that Flow Hive would actually work, having seen how much effort (and self-sacrifice) usually goes into collecting honey. The old-fashioned process for retrieving honey from the bees' pied a terre involves raiding the hive to get the frames that hold the honeycomb, spinning them in an extractor to separate the honey from the comb with centrifugal force, refining the honey to remove wax and dead bees (yes, dead bees), and finally donning the spaceman suit again to return empty frames to the hive.

.
Related: Best Flowering Plants For Honeybees

Flow Hive does it in three steps: Turn lever. Collect honey. Reset lever so the bees can refill the frame.

The designers are Stuart and Cedar Anderson, a father-son team based in rural Australia. Cedar is a third-generation beekeeper who has been collecting honey since he was 6. Cedar recruited his father to help with the design, which they've been working on for more than a decade and field-testing for the past three years.

How It Works

Instead of wooden, wax-covered frames, Flow Hive's BPA- and bisphenol-free plastic frames use a patented split-cell technology that creates channels within the hive. With the turn of a lever, the channels open up and allow honey to flow down into a trough and out of the hive into a waiting bucket. Unlike conventional hives, bees are undisturbed during the process and remain on the comb's surface during extraction. The potential result is that the honey has richer, more unique flavors because it comes straight from the honeycomb without any processing or heating. Flow Frames each hold about seven pounds of honey.

Some veteran beekeepers, however, object strongly to the Flow Hive, chiefly because they think the company's easy-breezy marketing oversimplifies beekeeping. They argue that turning beekeeping into an automated process will foster a disconnect between beekeepers and their bees, resulting in neglected hives if Flow purchasers don't realize how much hive maintenance is required outside of collecting honey. Some beekeepers also dislike plastic frames because bees naturally make wax comb without the assistance of a pre-started frame, and they believe the plastic may disrupt bees' communication.

Getting Started

Flow Frames can be used in a standard beehive with only minimal modification (directions are on their website), making it possible for longtime keepers to make the transition. Pre-orders for loose frames, flow boxes, and complete hives are being taken now (packages run from $260 to $670), and deliveries are expected to go out February 2016.

Until then, all the beekeepers I know will still don that wacky spacesuit to collect their honey—the good, old-fashioned way.

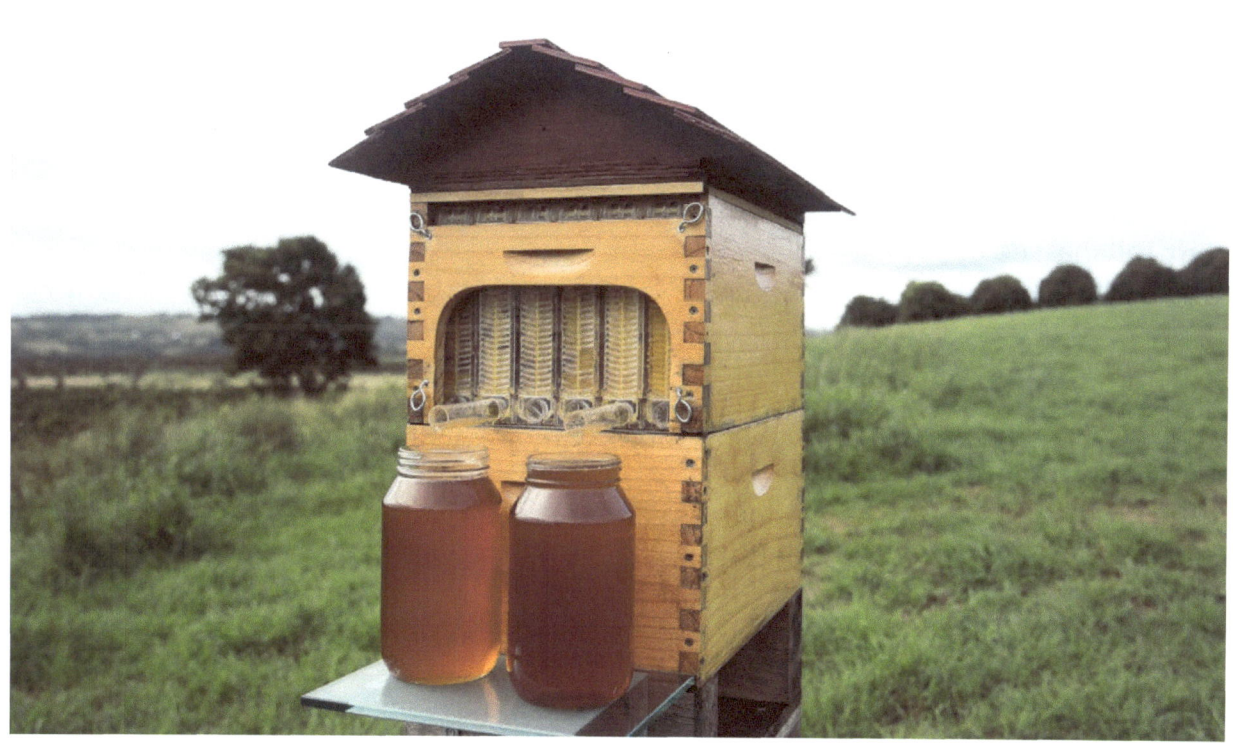

Politics And More

Captain of TransAsia Flight 235 shut off working engine after other failed: Report

Wow, pulled back the wrong side throttle."

These are the words of the captain of TransAsia Airways Flight GE235, eight seconds before the plane clipped a bridge and plunged into a Taiwanese river mere minutes after takeoff, killing 43 people on board.

The latest report by Taiwan's Aviation Safety Council into the February crash confirms that the captain of the ATR 72-600 turboprop aircraft mistakenly switched off the plane's working engine after the other lost power.

The biggest questions about Jeb Bush's tax returns

The 33 years of tax returns that Jeb Bush released this week included plenty of financial information about the former Florida governor.

He's worth as much as $22 million, paid an average effective tax rate of 36% over the course of more than three decades and saw his net worth explode to as much as $28.5 million since he left Tallahassee in 2007.

As if! 'Clueless' the musical is coming

One of your favorites '90s films will be "rolling with the homies" on Broadway.

Twenty years after "Clueless" hit movie theaters, director Amy Heckerling has confirmed to "Entertainment Tonight" that "Clueless: The Musical" is coming to the stage.

"I've written the, what they call the book, and it's a jukebox musical," Heckerling said.

A "jukebox musical" uses previously released and popular songs as opposed to songs specifically composed for the production.

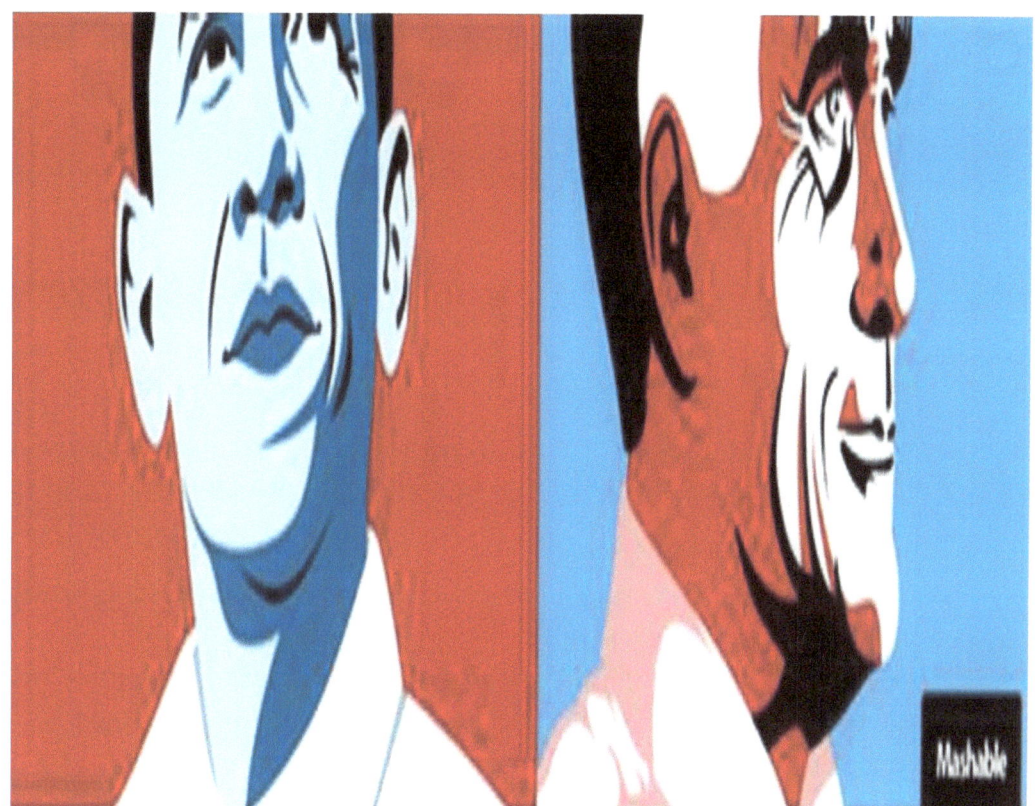

Politics Transformed

Politics: The who and what of politics

Dirty bomb: Just how worried should we be as ISIS seeks ultimate threat?

Last week, the news emerged that ISIS terrorists have reportedly obtained radioactive materials from hospitals and research facilities captured in Iraq with a view to developing a radioactive "dirty bomb."

Unsurprisingly, the prospect of ISIS dabbling with unconventional weapons has been greeted with considerable concern. The Iraqi government has appealed to the United Nations for international help to "stave off the threat" in this regard and Australian Foreign Minister Julie Bishop recently acknowledged that NATO countries are deeply concerned by the situation.

Religious extremism looms over Myanmar

The impact of Myanmar's repressive policy toward Rohingya Muslims was made clear in recent weeks with scenes of desperate people crammed into boats, an escalation of a miserable maritime flight in which an estimated 90,000 people have fallen prey to smugglers and traffickers since early 2014. The United Nations estimates that around 1,000 people have died on the way.

What is the value of an innocent life, Mr. Obama: $100K in a plastic bag?

In April this year, in the wake of the deaths of an American, Warren Weinstein, and an Italian, Giovanni Lo Porto, in a U.S. counterterrorism operation, U.S. President Barack Obama made an historic announcement, in which he said the following: "I take full responsibility for all our counterterrorism operations, including the one that inadvertently took the lives of Warren and Giovanni.

Sunday	Monday	Tuesday	Wednesday	Thursday	Friday	Saturday
July 2015						
			1	2	3	4
5	6	7	8	9	10	11
12	13	14	15	16	17	18
19	20	21	22	23	24	25
26	27	28	29	30	31	Notes:

Blank July 2015 Calendar Printable calendars available from www.blankcalendarprintout.com

July IS HERE!

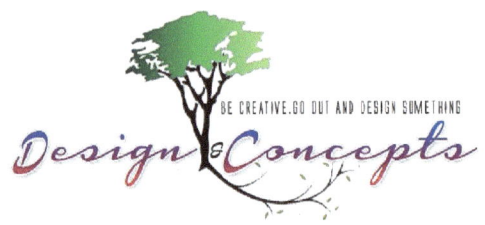

BE CREATIVE.GO OUT AND DESIGN SOMETHING

Join our mailing list
and get a free 1
month Subscription
to our magazine!

Owner

Design & Concepts L.L.C
Elizabeth Chavez
770-765-0687
www.designandconcepts.biz
www.lisabethdesignmagazine.com

Creativedesignconcepts@rocketmail.com

Place orders by email or contact

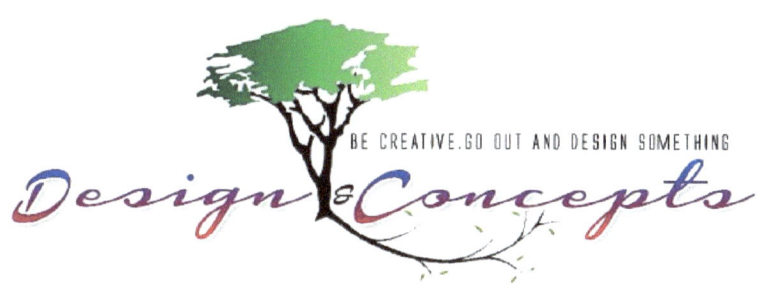

BE CREATIVE.GO OUT AND DESIGN SOMETHING

House of Lisabeths Design Magazine
We were started in 2013 as an independent magazine. Our focus is fashion, health and business. We pride ourselves in the design and diversity we offer.
Exclusivity
Our focus is fashion , health and business. Our fashion section includes tips and trends from all over! We also have a online blog that gets tons of clicks per day, check us out online at ......
Our business section is used for local or national business to place a Ad or listing of them selfs. We have total exclusivity In that they connect with not only our magazine but all of our networks simultaneously.
Our hope is to reach across the world along with Water 4 Kids International.
We plan to donate proceeds to this foundation. Our hope is to provide safe water for east Africa.
Check us out on line, Facebook, Twitter, Tumblr, Amazon, and our affiliates websites like Design & Concepts.

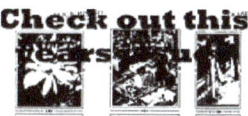

Get a 1 year subscription for $ 19.99———————— ☐

Personal Information
Name:_____   Email _____

Address_____ , Phone _____

City, State, Zip _____

Payment Enclosed————————- ☐
Pay Later————————————- ☐

Send To:

Design & Concepts

" Fill out above info and return to address given"
MIAMI
Liz Chavez
8369 NW 66 ST #3684
Miami, FL 33166

We also take check, cash and money orders.

Remember when you send for a subscription you get a free t-shirt that says "Lisabeth Design"

Thanks for supporting our fashion blog and Section!

Also with your subscription get a free Lisabeth Design T-Shirt

Available for Men and Women

Check out Design & Concepts Blog

I recognize that preaching the importance of social media to businesses is a little redundant. By now, buy-in to social media marketing is near ubiquitous, but I still find that many organizations have a difficult time quantifying the value they can achieve through the strategic use of social media.

While I certainly don't have a silver bullet response to help everyone understand the actual quantitative value of social media marketing, there are some incredibly compelling stats I'm going to share here to help you understand just how important social platforms can be to your business.

91% of people have gone into a store because of an online experience. (Source: Marketing Land)

This is a crazy statistic, but intuitively makes sense. Think about your own behaviour as a consumer. You probably spend a great deal of time researching the products and services you're interested in online before making a purchase decision. And why wouldn't you? With a world of information at your fingertips, it would be foolish to not research purchases online, read reviews, look up prices, get a sense for who you will be working with, determine how products are supported and serviced, and more.

Join the Cause!

Check out the " Design for Sick Kids Campaign"

Our Mission
In the beginning we wanted a way to show our passion for design.
But this project is turning to be more then that. With so many sick
kids and so much that we can give we thought about giving the gift
of design.

What We Need & What You Get
Here is what we need
1000 cards , either designed by you or who ever
A contribution as well to our campaign

The Impact
With every card made we will donate a dollar and that card to a local
hospital of our choice. So think about all the kids you can help by
creating there Christmas card or birthday card and also the contri-
butions that come with it.
Remember every card made we donate $ 1.00 to the cause
Also share your design with the people and get your picture taken
with the kids

Other Ways You Can Help Check out our websites
www.designandconcepts.net for more updates on more causes!

http://www.indiegogo.com/projects/design-a-card-for-your-kids/

Join the Cause!

Check out the "House Of Lisabeth Design Magazine- We are Here"

Our Mission
House of Lisabeth Design magazine is a new trendy magazine for fashion, trends, and business networking.

Hi, my name is Elizabeth Chavez I am the owner of Design & Concepts and am the editor and creator of " House of Lisabeth Design Magazine"

We are reaching out to you for a launch of our new magazine. For us it's important to get contributors from people who have faith in this magazine and want to help us launch it.

What were looking for is anything from 1 dollar to 100 dollars...The more people we reach the faster we will get to our goal.

Remember be creative go out and design something!

Also be sure to check us out on Facebook, Twitter, Amazon, Tumblr and our affiliate blogs , Lisabeth blog, and Design and Concepts blog

Also with your subscription get a free Lisabeth Design T-Shirt

Available for Men and Women

Design & Concepts Services

Www.designandconcepts.us

www.lisabethdesignmagazazine.com
www.lisabethfashionmagazine.us

Design & Concepts is an online service provider for design and advertising. We specialize in brochures logos and business cards as well as t shirts and sickies. We also do local advertising with in the community. Our prices vary with design but...

Our packages start at $55.00 per package!
Package includes : 200 prints
Gloss or matt finish is $10.00 per set/ per 200

Our Packages also include our Marketing Services, and Discounts on our Advertising Specials in our magazine, House of Lisabeth Design Magazine!

Also with your subscription get a free Lisabeth Design T-Shirt

Available for Men and Women

Design & Concepts Services:

Create various ads and place it on all social networks, web pages and create you tube videos to sell, demonstrate and promote your product

Also place your ad on any media source that is available We can take your campaign and place it on any other media resources you have available not just create a web presence awareness but really hit the market.

.We use digital media like

Email marketing, social network campaigns, print distribution, custom Web Design and SEO

New Words Every Business Owner Should Know

1. It's a paradigm shift = I don't know what's going on in our business. But we're not making as much money as we used to.

2. We're data-driven = We try not to make decisions by the seat of our pants. When possible, we try to base them in facts.

3. We need to wrap our heads around this = Gosh, I never thought of that. We need to discuss that....

4. It's a win-win = Hey, we both get something out of this (even though I'm really trying to get the best from you)

5. ROI [used in any sentence] = Look at me, I'm very financially-minded, even if I never took any finance classes in school

6. Let's blue sky this/let's ballpark this = Let's shoot around a bunch of ideas since we have no clue what to do

7. I'm a bit of a visionary = I'm a bit of an egomaniac and narcissist

8. I'm a team player/we only hire team players = I hope everyone on the team thinks this is a meritocracy, even though I'm the dictator in charge

9. Let's circle back to that/Let's put that in the parking lot/let's touch base on that later/let's take this off-line = Shut up and let's go back to what I was talking about

10. We think outside the box here/color outside the lines = We wouldn't know about how to do something innovative if it came up to us and bit us in the behind

FUNNY DEFINITION OF THE MONTH

Why Advertise with ....
House of Lisabeth Design Magazine
Lisabeth Fashion Magazine

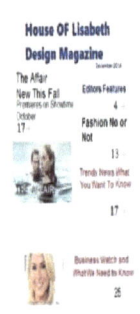 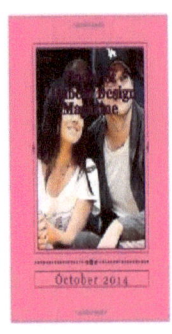 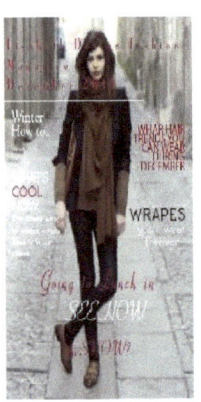

Our reach is growing, Our audience is picking us up, and our target audience is you!

Looking for classifieds, if interested submit your business and information and well help you out!

Liz:

LIZKELLY12@OUTLOOK.COM

Meet The Editor And Owner…..

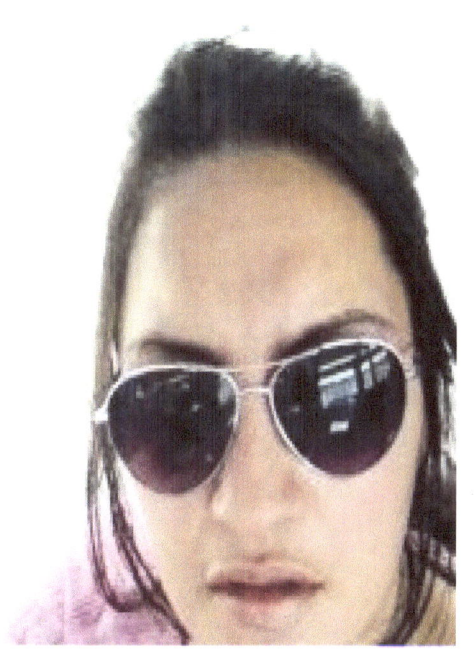 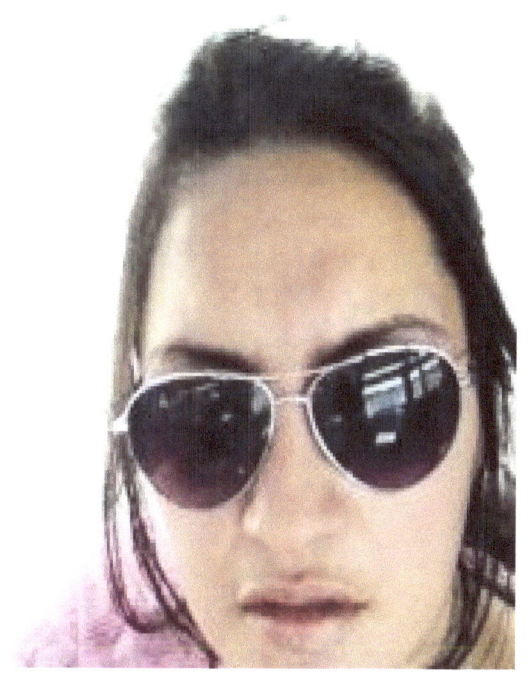

Elizabeth Chavez 28,,, Currently the owner of Design & Concepts LLC , and Editor of House of Lisabeth Design Magazine, and our newest Lisabeth Fashion Magazine. As an entrepreneur in her own field she manages both her business and love of de-signing in her everyday life. She works hard by involving all things that she can in many projects that she is involved with. One of her favorite is working on her fashion ideas blogging, posting or putting suggestions out all together.

Classifieds

JOB DESCRIPTION
We are looking for COMPETITIVE, SPORTS-MINDED Individuals for our marketing and advertising firm. The right person will love the thrill of a challenge and be excited to dive into new projects and sales.

MAVEN MARKETING GROUP

www.mavenmarketinggroup.net

We deliver flawlessly executed promotional sales programs and strategic marketing campaigns throughout the area. We provide our clients with a personal and professional solution for customer acquisition and increased sales/productivity.

JOB DESCRIPTION
Position Description: To assist current customers, potential customers, and fellow employees in the development, sales, installation, and support of hotel and resort software and hardware products developed and marketed by Multi-Systems, Inc. Proactively provides phone support for the diagnosing and resolving of computer software and hardware customer problems. Positively responds to customer service requests, inquiries and complaints working diligently to resolve and ensure maximum good will and meeting or exceeding customer expectations.

JOB REQUIREMENTS

Duties and Responsibilities:

90% Customer Support

Assist property personnel and fellow employees with technical support/product information issues in a professional, courteous and timely manner.

Classifieds

RN Clinical Supervisor Weekends (Home Health)
JOB DESCRIPTION
A very reputable Home Health / Hospice facility in Orange County is searching for an RN Weekend Clinical Supervisor. The Home Health facility is part of a large, financially stable Health Care organization in Orange County. Very competitive salary, compensation, benefits and work/life balance make this an incredible opportunity.

Job Summary: Supervises and coordinates the home health interdisciplinary team to insure competent, accurate and safe delivery of care to all patients. Clinical supervision of perfect care strategies; facilitates and insures quality initiatives and program implementation. Manages, maintains and sustains regulations, compliance of standards, and clinical care. Enforce mistake management, values, workplace standards, and policies of human resources.

Insurance Sales Agent
JOB DESCRIPTION

Schedule Required: Full time schedule, 40-hours per week based on operating hours of location assigned. May include evenings and rotating Saturday & Sunday hours. Specific schedules for location will be discussed at time of interview.
Special Info: AAA Mid-Atlantic was voted a 'Top Workplace for 2014' by it's Associates 8 years in a row! Come join an award winning organization valued for being a great place to work! Full Time Benefit Package includes: Medical, Dental, Vision and Prescription coverage; Paid time off; Continuing Education; 401k w/ company match & defined contribution; PLUS a FREE AAA Premier Membership. Other Benefits of this position will include: Generous Monthly & Quarterly Commissions; FREE Lead Generation; Paid trips for qualifying high producers; Paid training includes licensing & product knowledge; Plus, the opportunity to work as a sales professional in an entrepreneurial type work environment backed by the reputation and products AAA Mid-Atlantic has to offer.

**Why Advertise with
House of Lisabeth Design Magazine
Lisabeth Fashion Magazine**

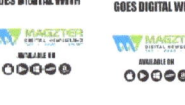

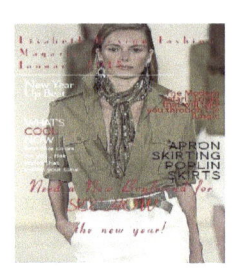

Our reach is out there growing !!!!

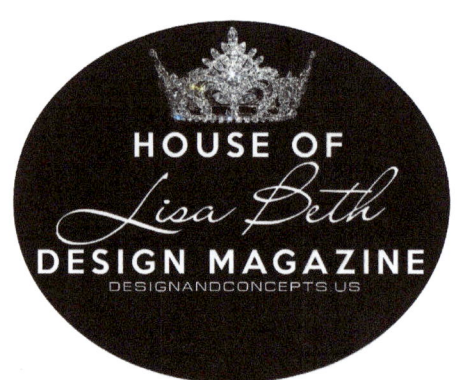

Lisabeth Fashion Magazine

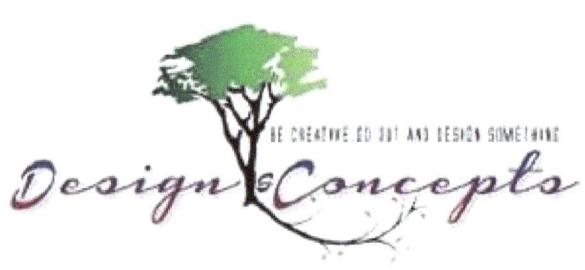

www.ingramcontent.com/pod-product-compliance
Lightning Source LLC
Chambersburg PA
CBHW050813180526
45159CB00004B/1646